OUR
GREAT AND
AWESOME
SAVIOR

OUR
GREAT AND
AWESOME
SAVIOR

Meditations For Athletes

Elliot Johnson
AND Al Schierbaum

Wolgemuth & Hyatt, Publishers, Inc.
Brentwood, Tennessee

The mission of Wolgemuth & Hyatt, Publishers, Inc. is to publish and distribute books that lead individuals toward:

- A personal faith in the one true God: Father, Son, and Holy Spirit;

- A lifestyle of practical discipleship; and

- A worldview that is consistent with the historic, Christian faith.

Moreover, the Company endeavors to accomplish this mission at a reasonable profit and in a manner which glorifies God and serves His Kingdom.

Published October 1991. First Edition.
Printed in the United States of America.
97 96 95 94 93 92 91 8 7 6 5 4 3 2 1

Unless otherwise noted, all Scripture quotations are from the Holy Bible, New International Version. © 1973, 1978, 1984 International Bible Society. Used by permission of Zondervan Bible Publishers.

Wolgemuth & Hyatt, Publishers, Inc.
1749 Mallory Lane, Suite 110
Brentwood, Tennessee 37027

Library of Congress Cataloging-in-Publication Data

Johnson, Elliot.
    Our great and awesome Savior : meditations for athletes / Elliot
Johnson and Al Schierbaum. — 1st ed.
        p. cm.
    ISBN 1-56121-069-0
    1. Athletes—Prayer-books and devotions—English. I. Schierbaum,
Al. II. Title.
BV4596.A8J64 1991
242'. 68—dc20   91-29015
                                                           CIP

Dedicated to the Lord Jesus Christ
"who was made a little lower than the
angels, now crowned with glory and
honor because he suffered death, so that
by the grace of God he might taste death
for everyone." (Hebrews 2:9)

CONTENTS

Foreword / *xiii*

Part 1: His Life Before "The Game":
   (The Savior Concealed in the Old Testament)

The Coach Who Always Was / *3*

Creator, Sustainer, and Sovereign Heir / *5*

The Promised Messiah / *7*

His Appearances Before Birth / *11*

Our Great High Priest / *17*

The Ark / *19*

The Isaac of Our Salvation / *21*

Joseph in Egypt / *23*

The Passover Lamb / *25*

The Smitten Rock / *27*

The Bronze Snake / *29*

The Curtain / *31*

Part 2: The Master Coach Enters the Stadium:
   (The Savior Revealed in the New Testament)

The Incarnation / *35*

Jesus: The God-Man / *37*

Jesus Grows Up / *41*

His Baptism / *43*

God's Anointed One / *45*

Jesus: His Temptation / *47*

Son of Man / *51*

Son of God / *53*

The Last Adam / *55*

Jesus Christ / *57*

Wonderful Counselor / *59*

Prince of Peace / *61*

Son of David / *63*

Lamb of God / *65*

Part 3: The Champion of Our Salvation:
    (The King Who Conquered Through Death)

His Death / *69*

His Resurrection / *71*

His Return to Heaven / *73*

His Present Work / *75*

His Message to His Team / *77*

Catching Away His Team / *79*

Our King / *81*

The Judge / *83*

Forever the Winner / *85*

Part 4: Game Plan of God's Man:
    (An Athlete's Guide Through John's Gospel)

The Word Became Flesh / *89*

Voice in the Desert / *91*

Choosing His Team / *93*

Taste of New Wine / *95*

Religion Made Easy / *97*

A Brand New Life / *99*

A Certain Outcome / *101*

The Well of Living Water / *103*

Meat and God's Will / *105*

Not Discouraged by Distance / *107*

Miracle at the Pool / *109*

Equal with God! / *111*

Reliable Witnesses / *113*

Training Table for Five Thousand / *115*

Training Camp at Sea / *117*

Bread That Satisfies / *119*

Dissension on the Team / *121*

Division in the House / *123*

The Right Time and Place / *125*

Irony and a Unique Man / *127*

Forgiveness: The Right Way Out / *129*

Light and Darkness / *131*

Who Is Your Dad? / *133*

A Bold Claim / *135*

Handicapped for God's Glory / *137*

Talk of the Town / *139*

The Real Blind Men / *141*

Our Master Coach / *143*

Voice of the Master Coach / *145*

Switching Positions for a Higher Purpose / *147*

Emotions of the Master / *149*

Glory and the Stone / *151*

Plot to Kill Jesus / *153*

Anointed with the Best / *155*

Welcomed to Death / *157*

The Highest Goal / *159*

Unbelief of a Nation / *161*

He Stooped to Conquer / *163*

Betrayed by a Companion / *165*

Jesus' Pep Talk / *167*

God's Way or No Way / *169*

The Spirit of Comfort / *171*

Producing for the Master / *173*

Expected Opposition / *175*

The Role Player / *177*

Strategy for the Second Half / *179*

Conference with the Coach / *181*

A Selfless Agent / *183*

The Unity That Speaks / *185*

The Cup of Our Salvation / *187*

Fickle Follower / *189*

Mock Trial of Righteousness / *191*

The Merciful in the Hands of the Merciless / *193*

Sacrificed for Us / *195*

Finishing What He Started / *197*

Setting the Stage / *199*

Victory from Defeat / *201*

Agony and Ecstasy / *203*

The Resurrection Revolution / *205*

That You May Believe / *207*

Fanatical for Jesus / *209*

Confidence in the Quarterback / *211*

About the Authors / *213*

FOREWORD

The athletic world is a world of comparisons. Teams compare the number of points scored against each other at the end of the game. Statistics measure proficiency of top scorers, rebounders, hitters, and pitchers by comparing one athlete's play with another's. Seasons are measured by comparing team victories with the competition.

The Apostle Paul made an interesting comparison in Philippians 3:8. He said, "I consider everything a loss *compared* to the surpassing greatness of knowing Christ Jesus my Lord . . . " (emphasis added). In other words, to know Jesus is so far superior to having a religion, an experience, an athletic thrill, a material possession, or any other relationship in life that there really is no comparison. We must know Him! We have no hope apart from knowing Jesus! Trophies, prestige, the wealth of this world, and all else pales in comparison to knowing Jesus Christ!

Paul added in verses 10–11: "I want to know Christ and the power of his resurrection and the fellowship of sharing in his sufferings, becoming like him in his death, and so, somehow, to attain to the resurrection from the dead."

Paul's goal was clear: that he might *know* Christ, deeply and lovingly. That is the goal of this book—that *you* might know the Lord Jesus Christ in a deep and intimate way and that you might become like Him. Knowing Him is the greatest goal ever set by any man, for to know Him is life eternal!

ELLIOT JOHNSON AND AL SCHIERBAUM

HIS LIFE BEFORE
"THE GAME"

The Savior Concealed
In the Old Testament

In the past God spoke to our forefathers through the prophets at many times and in various ways, but in these last days he has spoken to us by his Son, whom he appointed heir of all things, and through whom he made the universe.

Hebrews 1:1–2

THE COACH
WHO ALWAYS WAS

Read John 1:1–5

In the beginning was the Word, and the Word was with God, and the Word was God. He was with God in the beginning. Through him all things were made; without him nothing was made that has been made.

John 1:1–3

Man has a way of honoring ex-coaches and athletes who have contributed greatly to the world of sports. We put them in the Hall of Fame in an attempt to remember the past. We try to immortalize men like Bear Bryant, Vince Lombardi, and Babe Ruth, who are made into legends by those who revere their achievements. Often the legend becomes bigger than the man!

There is one hero who is every bit as big as His reputation. The Lord Jesus Christ fully deserves all the acclaim given Him and more. He is the beginning and the end of all things for all time. He is the Head Coach who has always existed.

Jesus is called the "Word" in Scripture. Why? In the Old Testament, when God (*Yahweh*) revealed Himself or His truth to the Hebrews, they so revered the name *Yahweh* that they refused to speak it, referring to the revelation as the *Memra*, or Word of God. Writing in the New Testament, John refers to Jesus as God's revelation, or Word to man. John writes that the Word, Jesus, is also the Creator of everything. Colossians 1:16 and Hebrews 1:2 confirm this truth. The Father designed His cre-

3

ation, and the Son created everything according to the design. Though Jesus is a distinct personality from the Father, He was and is always totally God. He is the beginning as well as the ending of all things (Revelation 22:13). Jesus Christ is eternal.

All who place their faith in Him become children of God, fit for His kingdom. Though Jewish leaders thought that all Jews were right with God because of God's covenant with Israel, it is not enough to be born a Jew (John 1:12–13). Nor is it enough to be born of Christian parents. One must be born *again* by the Spirit of the Living God (John 3:5–8). Everyone who is born again by faith in the eternal Son of God is made ready for fellowship with God. Have you placed your faith in this Eternal One?

Meditation Time-Out

1. How long has Jesus existed?
2. Why is Jesus called the "Word"?
3. How does one become right with God?

CREATOR, SUSTAINER, AND SOVEREIGN HEIR

Read Hebrews 1

. . . whom he appointed heir of all things, and through whom he made the universe.

Hebrews 1:2

T hough blessed with great influence, power, and wealth during their playing days, many pro athletes struggle horribly when they retire. Possible loss of income, the need to change professions, and the difficulty of maintaining self-esteem off the playing field cause great psychological conflict. As nine-year veteran Steve Watson of the Denver Broncos once said, "We all fear the end because we're not sure we can make it out there."

In contrast to men, who often base their identity on what they do, the Lord Jesus Christ never wavers in His purpose, direction, or commitment to His plan. He is not disturbed or frustrated with changing roles. He not only created all things, but He sustains them. Later, He will inherit everything because of who He is.

John writes that *through Him* all things were made (John 1:3, 10). All three members of the Trinity had a role in creation. The Father designed the creation; the Son created everything (Hebrews 1:2); and the Holy Spirit brought life to creation. Paul writes that Jesus Christ created all things (Colossians 1:16)—things in heaven, things on earth, visible things, invisible things, thrones, powers, rulers, and authorities. He created the heavenly sanctuary where He dwells, as well as the mountains, trees, rocks, and rivers of earth. He created animals, plant life, and every human being. He created oxygen and all other elements for the survival

5

of man. He created the galaxies (Hebrews 1:10). He created the hierarchy of angels, including Lucifer and all other angelic beings who fell from heaven because of pride.

Jesus Christ not only created everything, but He sustains them by His powerful word (Hebrews 1:3). He is the Ruler of creation (Revelation 3:14); therefore, He has every right to set down conditions and principles for its continuance. He holds everything together (Colossians 1:17). If it weren't for the power of Jesus Christ, all things would immediately disintegrate. If He withheld oxygen from man for a few seconds, man would quickly perish. We all depend upon Jesus Christ, whether we acknowledge and trust Him or not.

The Lord Jesus sovereignly directs His creation. He causes or allows all things that happen. Some things He *disallows* are good in themselves, while other things are evil. He *allows* many events—both good and evil—to happen for a greater purpose. The things He *causes* to happen are only good. He has always been sovereign, and He always will be sovereign over creation. He will see His plan fulfilled.

Because He has paid the price to redeem His creation from the curse of sin, He also fulfills His role as heir of all things. He is worshiped today by the host of heaven (Revelation 4:8–11; 5:11–14), and one day He will receive universal worship (Philippians 2:9–11).

Meditation Time-Out

1. How do you know Jesus Christ created everything?
2. How does Jesus sustain the universe?
3. What right does Jesus have to inherit all things?

THE PROMISED MESSIAH

Read Genesis 3

And I will put enmity between you and the woman, and between your offspring and hers; he will crush your head, and you will strike his heel.

Genesis 3:15

Major league teams often swing big, off-season trades in hopes of landing a "savior" for the franchise—someone who will lead the team to a championship. Sometimes the trade develops as planned, and sometimes it doesn't. Not many trades work out as well as the Dodgers' 1988 acquisition of Kirk Gibson from Detroit. Gibson enjoyed an MVP season and led Los Angeles to the World Championship. He was one "savior" that lived up to his advanced billing.

Jesus Christ is the promised Savior-Messiah of everyone who will trust in Him. He has never and will never disappoint us in His person or His performance. Immediately after man disobeyed the Holy God in Eden, God promised to provide a way back to fellowship with Himself. In Genesis 3:15, God said that the offspring of the woman, Jesus, would crush the head of the serpent, Satan. In the process, the heel of the offspring would be bruised. The crucifixion of Jesus Christ as payment for our sins fulfilled both promises. Satan was defeated by the blood of Jesus because a way back to God was established. He "struck the heel" of Jesus on the cross and was overcome when God raised Jesus from the dead.

Though Old Testament writers couldn't see clearly in looking *forward* to the coming of Messiah, in looking *backward*, we see they told

7

the story of Jesus' suffering in minute detail. Here is a sampling of fulfilled prophecies from the New Unger's Bible Handbook.

- He would be of David's family: 2 Samuel 7:12–16; Psalms 89:3–4, 110:1, 132:11; Isaiah 9:6–7, 11:1; Matthew 22:44; Mark 12:36; Luke 1:69–70, 20:42–44; John 7:42.

- He would be born of a virgin: Isaiah 7:14; Matthew 1:23.

- He would be born in Bethlehem: Micah 5:2; Matthew 2:6; John 7:42.

- His coming would be announced by an Elijah-like herald: Isaiah 40:3–5; Malachi 3:1, 4–5; Matthew 3:3, 11:10–14; Mark 1:2–3; Luke 3:4–6, 7:27; John 1:23.

- His mission would include Gentiles: Isaiah 42:1–4; Matthew 12:18–21.

- His ministry would be one of healing: Isaiah 53:4; Matthew 8:17.

- He would teach by parables: Isaiah 6:9–10; Psalms 78:2; Matthew 13:14–15, 35.

- He would die with criminals: Isaiah 53:9, 12; Luke 22:37.

- He would be buried by a rich man: Isaiah 53:9; Matthew 27:57–60.

- Even His dying words were foretold: Psalms 22:1, 31:5; Matthew 27:46; Mark 15:34; Luke 23:46.

- He would rise from the dead the third day: Matthew 12:40; Luke 24:46. No particular passage is quoted from the Old Testament for this. That He would rise from the dead is definitely quoted in Acts 2:25–32 and 13:33–35 from Psalm 16:10–11. Jesus said it was written that He would rise the third day (Luke 24:46). He must have had in mind Hosea 6:2 and Jonah 1:7, and Isaac being released from death the third day (Genesis 22:4).

- His rejection would be followed by the destruction of Jerusalem and great tribulation: Daniel 9:27, 11:31, 12:1, 11; Matthew 24:15; Mark 13:14; Luke 21:20.

- Jesus Himself realized that in His death He was fulfilling the Scripture: Matthew 26:54, 56.

What a promise God made to man in Genesis 3:15. And what exact detail was used by the writers to present Jesus' coming to earth. How wonderfully our Savior fulfilled the prophecies of a servant who suffered for the sins of mankind.

Meditation Time-Out

1. How does Genesis 3:15 demonstrate the sovereignty of God?
2. How is Satan defeated at the Cross?
3. How can anyone miss the Messiah?

HIS APPEARANCES BEFORE BIRTH

Read Genesis 12

The LORD appeared to Abram . . .

Genesis 12:7

R ecord books are extremely important to the avid fan. The docu-
mented achievements of past heroes spark the interest of people
around the world. Sports records provide a basis for measuring players
against themselves and against other players.

The record book of the Old Testament documents the fact that God
has always been vitally interested in affairs on earth. He is so interested,
in fact, that He appeared numerous times to help mankind in the fight
against evil. Most Bible scholars believe that the Lord Jesus Himself
appeared several times *before* He came as a baby in Bethlehem. They
have a name for these preincarnate appearances of Jesus: *theophanies*.
Let's look at several theophanies of Jesus from the record book of the
Old Testament.

When Abraham was called by God, he obeyed and left his home-
land. Genesis 12:7 says that God *appeared* to Abraham. In other words,
God materialized. God promised to give Abraham the land of Israel, and
Abraham built an altar to the Lord. Here we learn:

- God has a purpose on earth.

- God has a plan for each person. Some of us (in fact, all of us) are on
  "Plan B" since we've failed God because of incomplete obedience.
  But God never gives up and will still accomplish His purpose.

- God will go to great lengths to meet man.

11

In Genesis 16:1–16, Hagar, pregnant by Abraham and mistreated by Sarah, fled into the desert. The angel of the Lord, which many scholars believe was Jesus Himself, appeared to this Egyptian slave girl with the message to return to Sarah. Then He promised to make her son into a great nation. The son, Ishmael, would become the father of the Arabs. Hagar called the Lord "The God who sees me" (v. 13).

Later, when Abraham had sent Hagar away a second time (Genesis 21), the angel of the Lord (Jesus Christ) called to her from heaven (21:17). He reaffirmed His promise to a miserable and dying woman and child. God was with Ishmael (21:20) and fulfilled His promise to the letter. Here we learn:

- God cares about the outcast, the lowly slave, and her offspring.
- God is very protective of His good name. Every detail concerns Him. He promised blessing to Abraham's seed, and even though Abraham sinned by distrusting God's timing, the Lord took care of *all* Abraham's offspring.

In Genesis 18, the Lord Jesus and two angels appeared to Abraham, this time with two messages. The first message was that Sarah would have a son. Though Sarah laughed at the prophecy, she did indeed bear Isaac, through whom the world was blessed. The second message was one of doom for the cities of Sodom and Gomorrah because of their sin. Here we learn:

- God is faithful despite man's unbelief.
- God judges sin.
- God warns His righteous servants before sending judgment.
- God withholds judgment upon many because of the faithfulness of a few.

In Exodus 3:1–4:17, Jesus appeared to Moses in the burning bush with the command to go to Egypt and proclaim deliverance for Israel. Here we see:

- God is a holy God.
- God is concerned for His people (3:7–8).
- The Lord is angered by unbelief and obstinance (4:14).

In Numbers 22:22–24:25, the Lord Jesus appeared to Balaam, a rebellious prophet who would have pronounced a satanic curse on Israel.

Standing with drawn sword in front of Balaam's donkey, Jesus stopped his devious plan and altered his message. Balaam could only speak the words God gave him, words of blessing to Israel. Here we learn:

- God intervenes—sometimes dramatically—in the affairs of men.
- God can take the evil interests of ignorant prophets and turn them for His glory.
- God's plan is blessing for His people.

In Joshua 5:13–6:27, Jesus appeared to Joshua as he contemplated the attack on Jericho. He appeared with drawn sword to give Joshua instructions for taking the city. Here we learn:

- Jesus is the one we need in every circumstance.
- God has a higher purpose in mind than simply "choosing up sides" in battle.
- Victory comes by trusting God and doing things His way.

In Judges 2:1–5, Jesus appeared again to Israel with a message of the consequences of their disobedience. Because Israel had not broken down the altars of the Canaanites but had instead allowed the pagans to coexist with them, the Lord Jesus decreed that the Canaanites would continue to be a thorn in Israel's side and their gods would ensnare them. At this judgment, Israel wept bitterly. Here we learn:

- God will not tolerate disobedience in His people.
- The consequences of disobedience are severe.
- If we do not remove evil from our lives, it will eventually trap us.

In Judges 6:11–24, Jesus appeared to Gideon, one of the fearful Jews who was harassed by Midian. Every few months the Midianites would raid Israel and take whatever they wanted. Cowardly Gideon was threshing a small amount of wheat in a winepress, hiding from his enemies. Jesus appeared to Gideon, addressing him as a "mighty warrior" (v. 12). He sent Gideon to save Israel, infusing him with courage as he went. Here we learn:

- God sees us as we can be, not as we are.
- God is still there when we feel abandoned.
- God delivers us from overwhelming odds (Judges 7).

In Judges 13, Jesus appeared to Manoah's wife with the prophecy of the conception of a son, even though she was sterile. He gave specific directions on how to raise the boy and even reappeared to confirm the directions. The boy, Samson, was to have supernatural strength and would begin the deliverance of Israel from her enemies, the Philistines (13:5). He grew; God blessed him; and the Spirit stirred him to do great deeds (13:24–25). Here we learn:

- God has a sovereign plan for us before we are born.
- Supernatural power is available to those who are empowered by the Spirit of God.
- Holiness (being "set apart") unto God is crucial if we are to be used by God.

In Zechariah 1, 3:1–2 and 12:10–14, Jesus appeared to Zechariah in a vision to pronounce the return of the Jews from seventy years of captivity and the rebuilding of Jerusalem and the temple. He was riding a red horse, symbolic of judgment upon the enemies of Israel. Then Jesus appeared to rebuke Satan and provide a fresh start for the high priests of Israel (3:1–2). Later (12:10–14), Jesus predicted that the Jews would see Him as He is and would grieve bitterly for what they had done to their Messiah. Here we learn:

- God is never thwarted in His program.
- He disciplines His people severely.
- He takes vengeance on those who persecute Israel.

In Daniel 10, the glorified Lord Jesus Christ appeared to Daniel with a detailed prophecy of the end times. His appearance was similar to the one seen by John (Revelation 1). Not only was the future revealed to Daniel, but much truth about spiritual warfare (angels v. demons) was taught by the angel who appeared "like a man" (v. 16). The vision of the glorified Christ overcame Daniel and took his strength. His face turned pale, he was helpless, and he could scarcely breathe until the "angel" gave him strength (v. 18). Here we learn:

- The presence of the glorified Jesus is awesome to behold.
- Spiritual warfare is continually waged in the heavens.
- God has a plan for the future.

What an amazing record the books of the Old Testament contain. Jesus was there all along, guiding and sustaining His children throughout history. His care and concern predate His crowning achievement— the victory over sin and death on Calvary for the salvation of all men.

Meditation Time-Out

1. What is significant about the angel of the Lord in the Old Testament?
2. Which nation did God choose to bring Jesus into history as a baby?
3. How has Jesus supernaturally protected that nation?

OUR GREAT HIGH PRIEST

Read Genesis 14:17–20

You are a priest forever, in the order of Melchizedek.

Hebrews 7:17

S ome players set the standard for excellence at their position. Others, who fall somewhat short of the level achieved by these "prototypes," are merely considered "types," or secondary examples, of what is ideal in a player at a certain position. In our day, Lawrence Taylor and Mike Singletary are prototypical middle linebackers in the NFL. Jose Canseco is the prototype of a power hitter with speed in baseball. And Michael Jordan is the prototype NBA scorer. All others are just types of these men at their positions.

While Jesus Christ is the prototype for manhood, the Old Testament records numerous types, or pictures, of Him. While no picture of Jesus is a perfect illustration, each demonstrates a characteristic of God's wonderful Son who came to save the world. In Genesis 14, we read of an ancient king/priest of Jerusalem who blessed Abraham after his defeat of pagan kings. His name was Melchizedek, which means King of Righteousness. He flashes across the pages of Scripture so briefly that he is easy to overlook. Yet, this Gentile king knew God, served Abraham bread and wine, and was given a tenth of Abraham's plunder!

The Old Testment priests were members of the tribe of Levi. They had to offer sacrifices for their own sins (Hebrews 7:27), and being only human, could not serve forever.

Christ's function as high priest goes much further than the Old Testament model. Indeed, He made that model obsolete. He offered one sacrifice for all time. He mediates forever between God the Father and us, His children. His is a *permanent* priesthood because He always lives to intercede (Hebrews 7:25).

Only two people in Scripture are both king and priest—Jesus and Melchizedek. Chapter 7 of the letter to the Hebrews completes the picture. His name, "king of Salem," means "king of Peace." He had no recorded beginning or ending of life, and he remains a priest forever. He received tithes and gave blessing. Psalm 110:4 declares that the Messiah would be a priest forever "in the order of Melchizedek." Hebrews 7:16 announces that this is true on the basis of Jesus' indestructible life. Like the Son of God, Melchizedek remains a priest forever (Hebrews 7:3).

Meditation Time-Out

1. What do Jesus and Melchizedek have in common?
2. What is known of Melchizedek?
3. What is a "type"?

THE ARK

Read Genesis 6–8

*By faith Noah, when warned
about things not yet seen, in
holy fear built an ark to save
his family.*

Hebrews 11:7

The decisions of an umpire in baseball are usually final. A base runner is either safe or out, and a call either way can have a great effect on the game. Very seldom does an umpire change a call, even if he has made a mistake.

When God declares a person safe or out in the game of life, that decision is always final and always correct. Take the case of Noah and his family. God had warned the world that judgment in the form of a worldwide flood was coming. Why would God send a flood? Because the Lord saw how wicked men had become. He knew that every inclination of the thoughts of man's heart was only evil all the time (Genesis 6:5). So God commanded Noah, a righteous man, to build a 450-foot ark to save all who would come. For the 120 years of construction, Noah was a preacher of righteousness (2 Peter 2:5). God waited patiently for men to believe him (1 Peter 3:20). All they had to do was enter the ark of safety before the judgment came. But the heart of man was stubborn, and one day God shut the door of the ark so no one could open it (Genesis 7:16). Only Noah and his seven family members believed God and were saved. Judgment was slow, but it was sure and final.

God has promised never to flood the entire earth again, but He will bring judgment one day by fire (2 Peter 3:6–7). We must flee to Jesus to escape the wrath to come (1 Thessalonians 1:10). Jesus is our only ark of safety. As the ark was God's idea in Noah's day, Jesus is God's idea

19

to save whoever will trust in Him. As the ark endured the judgment of the flood, Jesus bore our judgment on the cross. As the ark was a place of safety, Jesus is a secure place for us. We can be eternally safe by trusting Jesus. Let us enter into the ark of our salvation—the Lord Jesus Christ.

Meditation Time-Out

1. How many people responded to Noah's invitation to be saved?
2. How will God judge the world the second time?
3. How can we escape judgment?

THE ISAAC
OF·OUR SALVATION

Read Genesis 22:1–19

*By faith Abraham, when God
tested him, offered Isaac as a
sacrifice.*

Hebrews 11:17

The Wally Pipp story has become a baseball legend. In 1925, the Yankee first baseman arrived at the ballpark with a terrible headache. When he asked the Yankee trainer for a couple of aspirin, manager Miller Huggins heard the conversation and said, "Wally, take the day off. We'll try that kid Gehrig at first today and get you back in there tomorrow."

"That kid Gehrig" did play—and play well. Wally Pipp never got his job back; he was replaced by the greatest first baseman of all time. Lou Gehrig played every day for fourteen years. He played in 2,130 straight major league games, setting an unapproachable record for endurance. What a substitute Gehrig was!

The account of Abraham's obedience to God in offering Isaac as a sacrifice clearly pictures our perfect substitute, the Lord Jesus Christ. He was a more perfect and enduring substitute than Lou Gehrig. As Abraham obeyed God, he experienced in a small way the agony the Father felt when He sent Jesus to the cross to die for our sins. Jesus was the substitute for us, as the ram caught in the thicket was the substitute for Isaac.

In the same way that Isaac was Abraham's only son, Jesus was the only begotten Son of God (John 3:16). The love of Abraham for Isaac (Genesis 22:2) pictures the love of God the Father for Jesus (John 5:20).

Abraham was to go to a mountain in the region of Moriah for the sacrifice. Years later, Solomon built the temple on Mt. Moriah and offered sacrifices there. Much later, Jesus was crucified on a mountain in the same region. It would be just like God to complete the picture with the sacrifice of His Son on the same spot.

As Isaac willingly carried the wood for his sacrifice, Jesus willingly carried the cross to the place of His sacrifice (John 19:17). As Jesus' priority was to do God's will (John 4:34), so Isaac was submissive to the will of his father. But as no picture of Jesus is perfect, neither is this one. The angel of God stopped Abraham from killing Isaac. A ram was finally offered in his place. When Jesus went to the cross, no one intervened. God forsook Jesus on the cross (Matthew 27:46) that we might never be forsaken. Though He had saved others, men said He could not save Himself (Matthew 27:42). In fact, He could have saved Himself, but if He had done so, none of us would have ever been saved (Matthew 26:52–54). He became our perfect substitute.

Meditation Time-Out

1. What penalty does your sin require?
2. Who paid the penalty for your sin?
3. What will you do about Jesus' substitution for you?

JOSEPH IN EGYPT

Read Genesis 37

You intended to harm me, but God intended it for good to accomplish what is now being done, the saving of many lives.

Genesis 50:20

In 1983, Ed Whitson injured a finger on his pitching hand. Unable to throw a curve or a slider, he developed another pitch, a palm-ball changeup, that made him more effective. His adaptation to the injury led to a great year in which he helped the 1984 Padres win the National League pennant.

Our sovereign God is better able to bring good things out of evil than a big league pitcher. Look at the life of Joseph, one of the most distinct pictures of Jesus Christ in Scripture. As Joseph was deeply loved by his father but rejected by his brothers, the Lord Jesus was loved by God and rejected by His Jewish brothers. Joseph was sold for the price of a slave; Jesus was sold for thirty silver coins. Joseph became a servant in Egypt; Jesus became a servant on earth. Joseph resisted temptation (Genesis 39); Jesus resisted Satan's most severe temptations (Matthew 4:1–11). Joseph was unjustly condemned; so was Jesus. Joseph was later elevated to a position of power to save the world from death. Jesus was exalted to a position of power and authority to save every man who comes to God through Him. In Acts 2:23–24, we have the parallel passage of Genesis 50:20. Speaking of Jesus, Peter says, "This man was handed over to you by God's set purpose and foreknowledge; and you, with the help of wicked men, put him to death by nailing him to the cross. But God raised him from the dead, freeing him from the agony of death, because it was impossible for death to keep its hold on him." Thank you, dear God! Thank you, Jesus!

Meditation Time-Out

1. What evil did God use in Joseph's life?
2. How did God use Jesus' sufferings for our good?
3. How has God turned evil into good in your life?

THE PASSOVER LAMB

Read Exodus 12

For Christ, our Passover Lamb, has been sacrificed.

1 Corinthians 5:7

One of the basic plays in baseball is the sacrifice bunt. The object is to advance a runner to the next base. The hitter must give up his chances for a safe hit by bunting the ball on the ground. The defense will surely throw the hitter out at first base, but in giving himself up, he has moved a runner into scoring position. A good sacrifice often leads to a victory!

When Jesus Christ gave His life on the cross, He became the perfect sacrifice for the sins of the world. The Righteous One gave up His life so that all who trust in Him might live. The Passover lamb, which the Israelites offered in Egypt, illustrates the sacrifice of Jesus. On the night prior to their release from slavery, each household took a lamb without blemish, killed it, and applied its blood to the doorposts and the top of the door frames. God commanded the destroyer to slay the firstborn of every man and beast in Egypt. But the Israelites whose houses were marked by the blood of the lamb were passed over and protected from destruction. In every household of Egypt there was death, either the death of the lamb or the death of the firstborn child. Great wailing was heard throughout the country because of this judgment, and Pharaoh finally released God's people from slavery to freedom.

The blood smeared on the doorposts pictures the cross of our Lord Jesus Christ. Israel was to keep this Passover festival every year as a reminder of God's deliverance. Similarly, we celebrate communion today as a reminder of the price of our freedom from sin. In the book of Hebrews, we read, "Without the shedding of blood there is no forgiveness" (Hebrews 9:22). "[We were redeemed] with the precious blood of Christ, a lamb without blemish or defect" (1 Peter 1:19).

Meditation Time-Out

1. What is the price of forgiveness?
2. Were the Jews impressed with the cost of their freedom?
3. Whose blood provides redemption for all believers?

THE SMITTEN ROCK

Read Exodus 17:1–7

Strike the rock, and water will come out of it for the people to drink.

Exodus 17:6

Dodger catcher Mickey Owen is remembered as the "goat" of the 1941 World Series. With two out in the ninth inning of game four, the Yankees were behind 4–3 with Tommy Heinrich at the plate. The Yankee slugger swung and missed for strike three on a pitch from Hugh Casey. But Owen let the ball get away, and the Yankees scored four runs to win, 7–4. Though everyone blamed Owen, the truth was that Casey had thrown an illegal pitch, a spitter, which fooled both batter and catcher.

While Israel was en route to the Promised Land, they camped at Rephidim. Finding no water to drink, the entire assembly blamed Moses and grumbled against him. Moses took the complaints to God. As usual, God was teaching Israel to trust Him, and He had the solution. He instructed Moses to take several leaders of the people and to approach the rock at Horeb. Moses was to strike this rock with his staff and water would be released for the entire nation to drink. Moses obeyed, and God provided.

The New Testament sheds more light on this rock. First Corinthians 10:4 says, "For they drank from the spiritual rock that accompanied them, and that rock was Christ." Jesus is the Rock. When He was smitten on the cross, He released every spiritual blessing necessary for salvation and godly living. He has given us the pure water of life. In John 4:14, Jesus said, "Whoever drinks the water I give him will never thirst.

Indeed, the water I give him will become in him a spring of water welling up to eternal life."

Years later, Moses was again faced with a water crisis in the wilderness. This time the nation was camped at Kadesh (Numbers 20:1–13). God gave Moses instructions to simply speak to a rock, and He promised to supply water. While the Hebrew word used for *rock* in Exodus 17:6 signifies low-lying bedrock (picturing the humility of the Savior), the word used in Numbers 20:8 pictures a high and exalted rock. Instead of obeying God, Moses struck this rock twice in front of the whole assembly. Though water did come forth, Moses had disobeyed God and taken glory for himself (v. 10). God's penalty to Moses was to give leadership to someone else, Joshua, who would lead Israel into the Promised Land.

What does the Kadesh experience teach us? We are to remember that Jesus Christ, our Rock, was crucified once for all time (Hebrews 9:26–28). When we are in need today, we need only speak to Him in prayer, for He has promised to fulfill all of our needs according to His glorious riches (Philippians 4:19). He is never to be crucified again or humiliated in any way. He is our Rock. He is our security. Let us rest in Him today.

Meditation Time-Out

1. How is Jesus like the smitten rock?
2. How do we approach Jesus today?
3. What price did Moses pay for disobedience?

THE BRONZE SNAKE

Read Numbers 21:4–9

So Moses made a bronze snake and put it up on a pole. Then when anyone was bitten by a snake and looked at the bronze snake, he lived.

Numbers 21:9

A minute detail cost Mark Martin the biggest fine in stock car history on February 25, 1990. After winning the Pontiac 400 in Richmond, Virginia, Mark discovered that the spacer between the carburetor and the intake manifold was one-half-inch too long according to NASCAR rules. He was fined $40,000 and penalized forty-six points in the season standings. A seemingly small thing proved very significant for Mark.

A small thing also had a great effect on the Israelites during their journey through the wilderness and vividly illustrates the healing, life-giving effect of the death of Jesus Christ. Much discouraged by the heat of the desert near the Gulf of Aqaba and with their food and water provisions, Israel griped against God and against Moses, their leader. The Lord sent poisonous snakes to discipline them for their impatience. (People who travel through the area say it is still infested by large snakes with fiery red spots and wavy stripes.) The snakes bit the Israelites, and many of them died. Realizing their sin of grumbling and discontent, those still alive confessed to Moses and to the Lord and requested prayer. God told Moses to "Make a snake and put it up on a pole" (Numbers 21:8). Anyone who was bitten would live if he would simply look at the snake on the pole.

29

Where did the power to be saved reside? Not in any bronze snake. It seemed like such a small, insignificant thing. Jesus explained, "Just as Moses lifted up the snake in the desert, so the Son of Man must be lifted up, that everyone who believes in him may have eternal life" (John 3:14–15). The bronze snake pictures the death of Jesus on the cross. Anyone who had the faith to simply look at the snake was healed and given life; anyone who will look to Jesus will be saved today.

The poison of sin brings death to all men today. We are all dead in trespasses and sins. But He became sin for us that we might have His righteousness (2 Corinthians 5:21). Jesus on the cross was not a pretty sight, but He brings life to all who will trust in Him. Will you look to Him today?

Meditation Time-Out

1. Who has the power to save and heal?
2. What is the requirement for salvation?
3. Why do you think God made the requirement for salvation so simple for us?

THE CURTAIN

Read Hebrews 10

Therefore, brothers, since we have confidence to enter the Most Holy Place by the blood of Jesus, by a new and living way opened for us through the curtain, that is, his body.

Hebrews 10:19–20

A good coach gives simple and clear directions to each member of his team. The goal is to help the player develop his potential and produce a winning effort. Every athlete must listen closely and obey instructions if he is to succeed.

In the Old Testament, our wonderful God gave most specific and clear directions on how to worship Him. Within His temple were three areas: an outer court, the Holy Place, and the inner Holy of Holies, where He promised to dwell. Only the high priest could enter this small room and then only once a year. He was to offer the blood sacrifice of animals to signify atonement for his sins and for the sins of the people and to express faith in God's promise of a true Redeemer/Messiah who would one day die for the sins of mankind. A thick curtain separated the Holy of Holies from the Holy Place. To go behind that curtain into the presence of the Living God was an awesome experience.

At the very moment Jesus died on the cross, God supernaturally split the curtain from top to bottom (Matthew 27:51), symbolic of the access we have to God through the blood of His Son. We are through with animal offerings (they never took away sin anyway—Hebrews 10:4) because only the offering of Jesus on Calvary removes all our sins. As the veil was torn in two, so His body was torn on the cross for us.

All believers are also "priests." All believers have free access to God by the blood of Jesus, His Son. Come boldly before Him and receive the grace so necessary for living in an evil world!

Meditation Time-Out

1. What kept man from God?
2. How was the "dividing curtain" removed?
3. What is our only means to enter the presence of the Living God?

PART 2

THE MASTER COACH ENTERS THE STADIUM

The Savior Revealed In the New Testament

The mystery that has been kept hidden for ages and generations, but is now disclosed to the saints. . . . which is Christ in you, the hope of glory.

Colossians 1:26–27

THE INCARNATION

Read 1 Timothy 3:14–16   *He appeared in a body.*

1 Timothy 3:16

O ccasionally a ballplayer plays so well that it seems he has no peer. Brooks Robinson, former third baseman of the Baltimore Orioles, was such a defensive player. He became the standard of excellence at the "hot corner." It was often said of Brooks that he played third base as if he "came down from a higher league."

Our Lord Jesus lived like He "came down from a higher league" because that's exactly where He did come from. He had no peer in any area. The embodiment of God in human form is called the *incarnation*. According to *Unger's Bible Dictionary,* the incarnation is "that gracious, voluntary act of the Son of God in assuming a human body and human nature." Many references confirm the incarnation of Jesus.

- "The Word became flesh and made his dwelling among us. We have seen his glory, the glory of the One and Only, who came from the Father, full of grace and truth." (John 1:14)

- "The first man was of the dust of the earth, the second man from heaven." (1 Corinthians 15:47)

- ". . . but made himself nothing, taking the very nature of a servant, being made in human likeness. And being found in appearance as a man, he humbled himself and became obedient to death—even death on a cross!" (Philippians 2:7-8)

- "Beyond all question, the mystery of godliness is great: He appeared in a body, was vindicated by the Spirit, was seen by angels, was preached among the nations, was believed on in the world, was taken up in glory." (1 Timothy 3:16)

- "Since the children have flesh and blood, he too shared in their humanity so that by his death he might destroy him who holds the power of death—that is, the devil. . . . For this reason he had to be made like his brothers in every way, in order that he might become a merciful and faithful high priest in service to God, and that he might make atonement for the sins of the people." (Hebrews 2:14, 17)
- "Therefore, when Christ came into the world, he said: 'Sacrifice and offering you did not desire, but a body you prepared for me.'" (Hebrews 10:5)

How did Jesus take on the form of man? The young girl Mary was a virgin who was made pregnant with Jesus by the Holy Spirit. This fulfilled the ancient prediction of Isaiah 7:14 which said, "The virgin will be with child and will give birth to a son, and will call him Immanuel." The literal meaning of *Immanuel* is "God with us" (Matthew 1:22–23). Matthew 1:18–25 clearly tells us that Mary had no sex with Joseph until *after* Jesus was born. What a miracle God performed when He conceived the body of the Lord Jesus in Mary's womb.

What changes were involved in Christ's incarnation? First, His dwelling place was changed from heaven to earth (John 6:38). Second, His material state changed from riches to poverty (2 Corinthians 8:9). Third, Jesus' position went from glory to obscurity (John 1:10, 17:5). Fourth, His status was changed from one of equality with God to that of a servant (Matthew 20:26–28; Philippians 2:6–7). All these changes were temporary. But another change—the change from the "form of God" to the "likeness of man"—was permanent. Today, He sits at the right hand of the Father making intercession for us. He knows us and can help us because He's one of us.

Meditation Time-Out

1. Define *incarnation.*
2. What does *Immanuel* mean?
3. What changes took place when Jesus came to earth?

JESUS: THE GOD-MAN

Read Romans 1:1–6

> *. . . regarding his Son, who as to his human nature was a descendant of David, and who through the Spirit of holiness was declared with power to be the Son of God.*
>
> Romans 1:3–4

In the game of baseball, a man is either safe or out. A pitch is a ball or a strike. A ball is hit fair or foul. The difference is not always readily apparent; there are some tough calls. There are some wrong calls by umpires, but there are only two choices, and you can't have it both ways.

But when we consider the nature of Jesus Christ, we have a unique case. While all other human beings are just that—human beings—Jesus Christ is *both* human *and* God at the same time. Of Him it can be said that He is simultaneously 100 percent God and 100 percent man. It is a great mystery how a person could be 100 percent of both. Yet, this union of God and man is clearly taught in Scripture.

- In the same passage, Jesus talked of driving out demons, healing people, and dying. (Luke 13:31–33)
- He was sleeping as a man moments before He calmed a storm as Lord of creation. (Matthew 8:23–27)
- He had foreknowledge of future events, but He needed a colt to ride. (Mark 11:1–6)
- As a man He hungered, while as God He cursed a tree and it withered. (Mark 11:12–14, 20–21)
- He wept in sorrow and then raised the dead. (John 11:35–44)

- As a man He suffered severe temptation, but as God He could not have fallen. (Hebrews 2:18; 4:15)
- He called Himself a man, and yet the Pharisees persecuted Him for His supernatural knowledge. (John 8:40)
- He was a man from heaven, but He rose from the dead. (1 Corinthians 15:21, 47)
- He had human ancestry but is God over all creation. (Romans 9:5)
- He is the crucified Lord of glory. (1 Corinthians 2:8)
- He was in very nature God but was found in appearance as a man. (Philippians 2:5–11)
- He is worshiped in heaven today as the Lamb who was slain. (Revelation 5:11–14)
- He dwells in our hearts by faith (Ephesians 3:17), and yet He has a body of His own. (Luke 24:35)
- He was from the beginning (John 1:1), and yet He was born a baby. (Luke 2:11)
- He is the Righteous One who died to bring us to God. (1 Peter 3:18)
- He lives forever as a permanent priest, making intercession for us. (Hebrews 7:24–25)

Can we fully understand Him? No. The finite cannot comprehend the infinite; our minds are too small. Can we believe Him? Yes. We can believe Him, because He cannot lie. He is fully God and fully man. He is recognizable as the Son of Man today (Acts 7:55–56). Jesus did not cease to be God when He became a man, nor did He cease to be a man when He returned to heaven (Hebrews 13:8).

What was the purpose of the incarnation? To bring God and man together. In the Old Testament, Job yearned for someone to arbitrate or mediate between himself and God (Job 9:32–35), but there was no one found to bring him close to the Father. Jesus came to join us to God by paying for our sin so we could approach God (1 Timothy 1:15). He tasted death for every man (Hebrews 2:9). He came to bring life—abundant and eternal life (John 6:51; 10:10).

Not only did Jesus come to bring us life, He also came that He might experience the same trials we experience and triumph over every one (Hebrews 2:14–18). Because He suffered when tempted, He is able to help us. He is our example of how to handle suffering and temptation (1 Peter 2:21).

Finally, Jesus' purpose was to reveal more completely the glory of God (John 1:14). He is the image of the invisible God (Colossians 1:15). Jesus said, "Anyone who has seen me has seen the Father" (John 14:9). In Jesus we see more fully the glory of God than in any other source. These are the purposes of His incarnation. He truly "came down from a higher league."

Meditation Time-Out

1. Why is Jesus not totally understandable to man?
2. Where can we find God's testimony about Jesus?

JESUS GROWS UP

Read Luke 2:41–52

And Jesus grew in wisdom and stature, and in favor with God and men.

Luke 2:52

The youngest player ever to play in the big leagues was fifteen-year-old Joe Nuxhall, who pitched for the Cincinnati Reds on June 10, 1944. When told to warm up, he was so tense that he tripped on the dugout steps and fell. Then Joe gave up five runs, five walks, two wild pitches, and two hits in two-thirds of an inning before being removed. He was sent to the minors, where he spent eight years maturing before returning to enjoy a fine career in the major leagues. He was a good pitcher who needed time to grow up.

Not much is known of the growing-up years of Jesus, but we do know that He grew in mind and in body. We know that stories of childhood miracles are false, for the Bible says that His first miracle was performed as an adult in Cana of Galilee (John 2:11). He was raised by Joseph and became known as "the carpenter" around Nazareth, his hometown (Mark 6:3). Because people were familiar with Him from His youth, they took offense when He manifested great wisdom and power in His miracles as an adult. They couldn't understand where He got His power, and they refused to believe He was God (Mark 6:4–6).

Luke records an incident when Jesus was twelve years old. While returning from their yearly Passover trip to Jerusalem, Joseph and Mary noticed that Jesus was not among their fellow travelers. They retraced their steps to Jerusalem, which took one day, and spent three more days searching the city for Him. They found Him in the temple courts listening, asking questions, and teaching the religious leaders of Israel.

41

"'Why were you searching for me?' he asked. 'Didn't you know I had to be in my Father's house?'" (Luke 2:49). As a young man, Jesus had His priorities in order, yet He still had misunderstandings with His parents. They did not understand Him or His desire to "be about His Father's business." His reply to His parents reveals that there was never a time when He did not know who He was, who His real Father was, or why He had been born into the world. However, Jesus was always obedient to His earthly parents (v. 51), and He grew intellectually, physically, spiritually, and socially (v. 52).

Education was important to Jesus. Jesus spoke Aramaic, the language of the day. But He evidently knew Hebrew because He quoted directly from the original Hebrew scriptures. We deduce He knew Greek as well, or He could not have spoken to strangers like the centurion, with Pilate, or with those Greeks who questioned Him the last week of His life.

As a teenager, Jesus didn't race His chariot through the streets of Nazareth, endangering the lives of others. He wasn't a nerd, nor was He a conceited jock who gloated and pointed fingers with every touchdown He scored. He was popular because He was wise, not because He compromised His convictions of right and wrong. Through the trying years of growing up, in His job at the carpenter's shop, and in every relationship, Jesus lived His life on an even keel. He had a good reputation with both God and men.

Meditation Time-Out

1. How is Jesus different from some of today's so-called heroes?
2. Is it possible to live a pure life while growing up?
3. How was Jesus regarded as He grew up?

HIS BAPTISM

Read Matthew 3:13–17

When all the people were being baptized, Jesus was baptized too. And as he was praying, heaven was opened and the Holy Spirit descended on him in bodily form like a dove. And a voice came from heaven: "You are my Son, whom I love; with you I am well pleased."

Luke 3:21–22

E veryone recognizes the distinctiveness of New York Yankee pin-stripes, the silver and black of the L. A. Raiders, or the green and white of the Boston Celtics. Their uniforms have become famous. The uniform identifies a player with his team and makes him clearly seen as one of them. That's why teams wear different colors and styles. They want to remain distinct from each other, to create an identity for their organization.

Our Lord Jesus wanted to identify with us. Therefore, He insisted that John baptize Him in the Jordan River. At first John refused to baptize Jesus, for John was baptizing as a symbol of confession of sin and repentance. Jesus, being perfect, had no need to confess anything nor to repent of anything. But Jesus wanted to be baptized as an outward sign of identification with mankind. It was part of Jesus' humbling Himself to come near to us. Today, He asks Christians to be baptized as an outward symbol of the change He has wrought in them. We are to identify with Him as He identified with us.

43

As Jesus was baptized, God the Father broke into the scene in three ways: heaven was opened; the Holy Spirit descended upon Jesus in bodily form like a dove; and the voice of God proclaimed Jesus' sonship and His acceptability to the Father. All three persons of the Trinity were visibly or audibly present at once! In one dramatic moment, the Spirit of God equipped the Son of God for the job He came to do. Our Savior was now ready to be proved sinless—capable of redeeming the race with whom He had so closely identified.

Meditation Time-Out

1. What is the significance of baptism?
2. Why was Jesus baptized?
3. Why did John hesitate to baptize Jesus?

GOD'S ANOINTED ONE

Read Acts 10:34–48

. . . how God anointed Jesus of Nazareth with the Holy Spirit and power, and how he went around doing good and healing all who were under the power of the devil, because God was with him.

Acts 10:38

Jackie Robinson was specifically chosen by Branch Rickey to break the "color line" in professional baseball. Signed in 1946 from the Negro Leagues, Jackie was chosen for his great talent and strong character. Mr. Rickey's search had spanned the globe, and Jackie was the one he wanted. Furthermore, Rickey grilled Robinson in preparation for the abuse he would receive from white players and fans. "Are you looking for a Negro who is afraid to fight back?" Jackie asked. Rickey exploded, "I'm looking for a ballplayer with guts enough *not* to fight back." Jackie Robinson knew he had to "turn the other cheek." Chosen for his character and driven by a great cause, Jackie Robinson represented the black athlete with dignity and class, opening the way for thousands of others in the world of sports.

Our God has a way of setting aside a man for special purposes greater than the desegregration of baseball. In the Old Testament, His choice was symbolized by pouring oil upon the head of the person. This was called *anointing*.

Prophets, priests, and kings were all installed into office this way. It was a serious offense to try to harm the one whom God had thus anointed!

Jesus Christ is God's Anointed One, chosen for the special task of redeeming and securing mankind for God the Father. He is our prophet, our priest, and our king. God anointed Him, not with oil, but with the power of the Holy Spirit, as a means of accomplishing His task. Because of the anointing of the Spirit, Jesus went around doing good and healing those under Satan's power. He was able to do these things because God was with Him (Acts 10:38).

"God with us" is a great definition of *anointing* in our day. Second Corinthians 1:21–22 tells us that He has anointed us, set His seal of ownership on us, and put His Spirit in our hearts as a deposit guaranteeing what is to come! We are as chosen as was Jackie Robinson! Our future is secure because of His anointing. First John 2:20 says we know truth because of His anointing. First John 2:27 says that this anointing teaches us all things! Our special task of glorifying God is possible because we have an anointing from the Anointed One.

Meditation Time-Out

1. What is an anointing?
2. How did God anoint Jesus?
3. What were the results of Jesus' anointing?

JESUS: HIS TEMPTATION

Read Matthew 4:1–11

Jesus, full of the Holy Spirit, returned from the Jordan and was led by the Spirit in the desert, where for forty days he was tempted by the devil. He ate nothing during those days, and at the end of them he was hungry.

Luke 4:1–2

W hen a rookie breaks into the big leagues, he must prove himself capable of competing at a higher level. The parent club believes in him, or they wouldn't have promoted him; but it takes some time to prove whether he is, in fact, a big league player.

Jesus went through a period of time in which He proved Himself as the sinless Son of God, able to defeat Satan and save the world. His period of great testing was in the wilderness just after being baptized and filled with the Holy Spirit. In fact, the Spirit led Him into mortal combat with Satan. Tradition says the site was Quarantania, a fifteen-hundred-foot mountain which lies in a barren wilderness six to eight miles west of the Jordan, where He was baptized. For forty days, Jesus allowed Satan to test Him so that His sinlessness might be revealed. He was tempted in every way as we are (Hebrews 4:15). He suffered while being tempted (Hebrews 2:18). But the certain outcome of His victory over temptation established His personal authority over Satan at the very beginning of His ministry. While the first Adam lost everything by falling into Satan's snare in a beautiful garden, the last Adam, Jesus, regained everything by total dependence upon His Father in the wilder-

47

ness. He did it by the Word of God, specifically quoting from Deuteronomy—the book of obedience (Deuteronomy 8:3; 6:13, 16).

At the baptism of Jesus, Satan had heard God say of Jesus, "You are my beloved Son." The devil's first thrust was to try to make Jesus rely on self instead of God to meet His needs. "'If you are the Son of God,' Satan said, 'tell these stones to become bread'" (Matthew 4:3). The round, flat stones must have already resembled the flat bread cakes of Palestine to the starving Jesus. Since Jesus was in the desert by God's will, His circumstances were God appointed. To gratify His physical desires would be to elevate the personal satisfaction of His appetite above obedience to the will of God. Jesus had supernatural power, but He had agreed to take on man's limitations. If He supernaturally saved Himself, He would disqualify Himself as man's representative and as Savior. He trusted His physical life entirely to His Father, quoting Deuteronomy 8:3: "Man does not live on bread alone, but on every word that comes from the mouth of God" (Matthew 4:4). Jesus recognized that obedience was greater than self-gratification. While the first Adam fell by eating (and we often sin that way), Jesus took control over the physical desire for food.

The second thrust of Satan was to get Jesus to claim recognition by presuming upon God's protection. Satan led Jesus to the city of Jerusalem. Jesus willingly followed to allow Satan to execute his "Plan B." At daybreak, when a crowd of early worshipers would be welcoming a new day in prayer, they arrived at the pinnacle of the temple. The devil challenged Jesus to jump off the temple into the courtyard of worshipers below, proclaim Himself Messiah, and receive instant recognition and acceptance. With the devil's inspiration, the crowd would accept this miracle and rally behind Jesus. Satan even quoted Psalm 91:11–12: "He will command his angels concerning you, and they will lift you up in their hands, so that you will not strike your foot against a stone" (Matthew 4:6). The devil left out, "to guard you in all your ways." For Jesus to take a flying leap off the temple would have been to presume upon God's protection. It was not in God's will nor in His way for Jesus to be recognized in this manner, and Satan knew it. Jesus resisted by reminding Satan that Deuteronomy 6:16 tells us, "Do not put the Lord your God to the test" (Matthew 4:7). To follow Satan's suggestion would have been to test God's protection by acting outside His will. God promises to protect us *from* sin, not *in* sin. Jesus proved Himself superior to this temptation, too.

Satan saved his worst temptation for last. His "Plan C" involved taking Jesus to the great mountain. There, one could see for miles. On one side could be seen caravans passing through the land. On another side were fortified cities, and to the west was the great ocean. It was an awesome sight, representing all the wealth and kingdoms of the earth. In an instant, Satan caused a vision of all the peoples of the world submitting to Jesus' authority (Luke 4:5). Satan held this power, for God had given dominion to the first Adam, and he had forfeited it all to Satan in Eden. Satan is the god of this age who blinds the eyes of unbelievers (2 Corinthians 4:4). He covets the worship due to God more than anything. He promised to give all his authority for that worship. Jesus was offered the kingdom on easy terms, without going to the cross. His reply? *"Worship* the Lord your God and *serve* him only" (Luke 4:8, emphasis added). Jesus knew what the first Adam had not known: To worship Satan is to serve Satan. If He bowed to Satan, the supreme authority would still be Satan's. Jesus would have rendered Himself powerless to save us, and Satan knew it. The devil's lures are always a sham.

Jesus resisted Satan, proved Himself perfect, and then dismissed him. Luke says the devil left Jesus until a more opportune time. That time was at the Cross (John 14:30–31). What do we learn from Jesus' temptations? Among other things, we see the following:

1. We have a Savior who is holy, blameless, pure, and set apart from sinners. (Hebrews 7:26)
2. Jesus was tempted in all ways we are tempted (Hebrews 4:15; 1 John 2:15). First, He was tempted by the lust of the flesh, for fresh bread to a starving man is more tempting than a woman in a bikini to a man on a deserted island. Second, Jesus was tempted by the pride of life. The crowds in Jerusalem would have adored Him as their hero if He had done a Superman leap off the temple. Third, He was tempted by the lust of the eyes. How appealing to rule the world empires, especially with no cross superimposed over the throne.
3. Jesus withstood severe temptation. We have His power in us, so we can stand in the face of temptation also.

4. He knows how we feel when tempted, for He has been there.

5. Jesus is mightier than Satan. Satan could not force Him to eat bread, push Him off the temple, or demand worship. He could only suggest these things.

6. Scripture is vital in resisting temptation. Jesus replied, "It is written" to all of Satan's suggestions.

7. Temptation is not a sin. Jesus was tempted by Satan. Only yielding is sin.

8. Hard times do not mean we are out of God's will. Jesus was led of the Spirit to the wilderness to be tested.

9. We are tested by God, but we must not test God (Matthew 4:7). To test Him implies we cannot trust Him. But if we know He is trustworthy, a test is unnecessary.

10. Satan has power, position, and wealth to give to those who bow to him, but his promises are a sham. The end is death.

11. Either God or Satan is the Lord of our personal kingdoms. To build a kingdom on earth without Jesus Christ as Head is to worship Satan.

12. Angels ministered to Jesus after His ordeal. If they were near Him on earth, they also are near to help us.

Could Jesus have fallen to Satan's temptations? No, because He was God. As God, He could not fall, so as man He would not fall. We fall to temptation because we are drawn by lusts and enticed (James 1:13–14). But there was nothing in Jesus, no sin nature, to even remotely lure Him to sin. The devil's schemes only proved Him perfect. Though the temptations were much greater than those we ever experience, Satan had attempted the impossible.

Meditation Time-Out

1. What did Jesus' temptations prove?
2. What power do you have to resist temptation?
3. What excuses do we have for yielding to temptation?

SON OF MAN

Read Daniel 7

*For the Son of Man came to
seek and to save what was lost.*

Luke 19:10

D ynasties are rare in sports today. There are no dominating franchises
like the great Yankee team of the past or the Packers under Vince
Lombardi. Probably the Los Angeles Lakers came as close to being a dynasty as any team of the 1980s, but even their reign was limited.

Even the political world has seen a collapse of dynasties with the
demise of worldwide communism. It remains to be seen whether there
will be a resurgence. We do know that there have been great world
empires in history. These were predicted before they came into being.
And we know that a permanent dynasty is on the horizon, for God gave
Daniel a preview. He wrote that one "like a son of man" was coming to
rule (Daniel 7:13–14).

It was revealed to Daniel that the kingdom ruled by one "like a son
of man" would not be like the four preceding temporary kingdoms. Each
of the others was conquered and divided. But His kingdom would rule
all peoples of the earth and would be everlasting, never being defeated
or coming to an end. Who is the Son of Man who would rule this dynasty? He is none other than our Lord Jesus Christ!

In the Old Testament, the title "Son of Man" was applied to an individual (Ezekiel 2:1) or to mankind in general (Psalm 8:4). Yet, the Hebrews
saw the Daniel passage as relating to the Messiah, the anointed king. The
Lord Jesus applied this title to Himself. First, He will return to set up His
reign on earth. He said, "Men will see the Son of Man coming in clouds
with great power and glory" (Mark 13:26). Jesus referred to Himself as the

51

Son of Man of Daniel's vision. Just prior to His crucifixion, Jesus was on trial before the chief priests and the council, and they asked Him,

> "Are you the Christ, the Son of the Blessed One?" "I am," said Jesus. "And you will see the Son of Man sitting at the right hand of the Mighty One and coming on the clouds of heaven." (Mark 14:61–62)

Again, Jesus was referring to Daniel's prophecy.

Second, "Son of Man" is a title revealing Jesus' suffering as a man. The Jews had a tough time accepting Him because they were looking for a mighty warrior instead of a gentle servant. Jesus came to set up a kingdom, but it was to begin as a spiritual kingdom in which sin, Satan, and death would be defeated. Many of Jesus' references to Himself as the Son of Man had to do with suffering and rejection. After Peter confessed that Jesus was the Christ, the Scripture says, "He then began to teach them that the Son of Man must suffer many things and be rejected by the elders, chief priests and teachers of the law, and that he must be killed and after three days rise again" (Mark 8:31).

Third, the name "Son of Man" reveals the authority of God. When Jesus was approached by a paralytic man, He told the man that his sins were forgiven. Some scribes heard this and said to one another, "Why does this fellow talk like that? He's blaspheming! Who can forgive sins but God alone?" (Mark 2:7). Jesus responded, "'But that you may know that the Son of Man has authority on earth to forgive sins. . . .' He said to the paralytic, 'I tell you, get up, take your mat and go home' " (Mark 2:10–11). Jesus' healing of the paralytic and others confirmed His Messiahship and proved that He had the authority of God.

Not only did the Son of Man have the authority to forgive sins, but He was also Lord of the Sabbath (Mark 2:27). He is the only one who can save a person from his sin. Being the Son of Man meant that Jesus had divine authority to do what only God could do.

"Son of Man" was Jesus' favorite title for Himself. He is destined to rule the world. Yet, this title reveals the humility, suffering, and rejection He experienced.

Meditation Time-Out

1. Where was the title "Son of Man" first used?
2. What does this title signify?
3. What title did Jesus most frequently use for Himself?

SON OF GOD

Read Mark 1:9–12

And a voice came from heaven: "You are my Son, whom I love; with you I am well pleased."

Mark 1:11

The year 1989 saw history being made in baseball. It was the first time a father and a son played simultaneously in the major leagues. Ken Griffey, Jr., the nineteen-year-old son of Ken, Sr., started for the Seattle Mariners, while his thirty-nine-year-old father was re-signed by the Cincinnati Reds. The physical skills of the father were evident in his son, and Ken, Jr., seemed destined for stardom.

The Bible makes it clear that Jesus Christ is the only-begotten Son of God, unique among men in all His attributes. As God's Son, Jesus possesses the very nature of His Father. How did this happen? The angel Gabriel foretold it to Mary: "The Holy Spirit will come upon you, and the power of the Most High will overshadow you. So the holy one to be born will be called the Son of God" (Luke 1:35). Jesus came to earth as man, but He remained God, for God was His Father!

Many times Jesus spoke of God as His Father. In Luke, Jesus revealed the unique knowledge the Son and the Father have of each other:

All things have been committed to me by my Father. No one knows who the Son is except the Father, and no one knows who the Father is except the Son and those to whom the Son chooses to reveal him. (Luke 10:22)

In John 17:5, Jesus prayed for His Father to glorify Him with the glory He had before the world began. Even demons proclaimed the truth of Jesus as the Son of the Most High (Mark 3:11; 5:7). There is no doubt from Scripture that Jesus is God's Son.

As God's Son, Jesus has a special relationship with the Father. It is a unique relationship that no man or woman can ever have, though we are made sons and daughters by adoption when we trust Him as Savior. In Romans we read, "Those who are led by the Spirit of God are sons of God" (Romans 8:14). And in Acts 17:28, Paul affirmed to the Stoics and Epicurians of Athens that we are offspring of God by creation. So, God is the Father of all men by creation, and He has a special relationship as Father to all who are born again by faith. But Jesus is the only Son of God who was with Him from eternity and was sent by God to be born of a woman at just the right time (Galatians 4:4). Because Jesus is God's Son, He can fulfill the role of Messiah to the whole world.

Meditation Time-Out

1. How is Jesus' relationship to the Father unique?
2. In what sense are all men "sons" of God?
3. In what sense are only believers "sons" of God?

THE LAST ADAM

Read 1 Corinthians 15:34–58   *So it is written: "The first man Adam became a living being"; the last Adam, a life-giving spirit.*

1 Corinthians 15:45

I n 1987, John Lucas of the Milwaukee Bucks realized the negative effect he had on others because of his addiction to alcohol and drugs. Lucas reveals how his four-year-old daughter held cigarette ashes to her nose, apparently mimicking the time she saw him snorting cocaine. "I've hurt a lot of my friends and my family," said Lucas, "and I'm humiliated by that."

No man has had a more negative effect on others than the first man, Adam. From the very moment he disobeyed God, death crashed his garden party with Eve. In Romans we read, "Therefore, just as sin entered the world through one man, and death through sin, and in this way death came to all men, because all sinned" (Romans 5:12). Adam's sin has affected every person who ever lived on this earth. Because of Adam, we all have inherited a sin nature, we are all condemned because of that sin, and we must all die. While we cannot blame Adam for our personal sin, Adam has passed on the sin nature and the death penalty to every human being. Adam's sin of disobedience had a universal effect.

By contrast, the obedience of Christ, the last Adam, also had a universal effect. The gift Christ brought to the world is in such contrast to what Adam brought that Paul says, "For as in Adam all die, so in Christ all will be made alive (1 Corinthians 15:22). Adam was from the earth and made of dust. He was the first human being. But Christ is from heaven and able to give a spiritual birth and a heavenly home to all who call upon His name. Christ completely reversed the consequences of Adam's fall. In Adam, mankind is guilty of sin, which brings about death, judgment, and condemnation. But in Christ, we receive justification and righteousness, which lead to eternal life.

The sin of the first Adam infected all men, while Jesus' death was for the redemption of the whole world (John 3:16). While the benefit of His death is available to everyone, only those who actually receive Him by faith receive forgiveness and eternal life (Acts 4:12). When a believer is "born again," he is born into the kingdom of God. The spiritual realm of life is opened to him. Paul says,

> You, however, are controlled not by the sinful nature but by the Spirit, if the Spirit of God lives in you. And if anyone does not have the Spirit of Christ, he does not belong to Christ. But if Christ is in you, your body is dead because of sin, yet your spirit is alive because of righteousness. And if the Spirit of him who raised Jesus from the dead is living in you, he who raised Christ from the dead will also give life to your mortal bodies through his Spirit, who lives in you. (Romans 8:9–11)
>
> We have not received the spirit of the world but the Spirit who is from God, that we may understand what God has freely given us. (1 Corinthians 2:12)

Because of Jesus, we can become children of God (John 1:12); we are partakers of the divine nature (2 Peter 1:4); and we have the mind of Christ (1 Corinthians 2:16). What a difference the last Adam makes! Let us honor Him above all men!

Meditation Time-Out

1. What happened as a result of the decision of the first Adam?
2. What did the last Adam achieve?
3. How do men "participate in the divine nature"?

JESUS CHRIST

Read Acts 4:5–22

It is by the name of Jesus Christ of Nazareth, whom you crucified but whom God raised from the dead, that this man stands before you healed. He is "the stone you builders rejected, which has become the capstone." Salvation is found in no one else, for there is no other name under heaven given to men by which we must be saved.

Acts 4:10–12

S ome names seem to perfectly fit a person for his work. For example, a guy named Bronco Nagurski certainly does not become a world famous pianist but a football player! Rocky Marciano is the perfect name for a world boxing champion. Henry Wadsworth Longfellow could only have been a writer. Pee Wee Reese is the perfect name for a shortstop, and Bo Jackson is the perfect name for a football player, a baseball player, a track star, or anything else you want him to play! Bo knows sports.

If names describe people, the greatest example of a name fitting a person is the name given to our Savior, Jesus Christ. Matthew records the message God spoke to Joseph in a dream. He said, "She will give birth to a son, and you are to give him the name Jesus, because he will save his people from their sins" (Matthew 1:21). When Simeon saw the baby Jesus he exclaimed, "For my eyes have seen your salvation" (Luke 2:30). The name *Jesus* wasn't a name that God the Father just picked out of a hat. *Jesus* comes from the Hebrew name *Joshua,* which means "Yahweh is help" or "the Lord saves." Jesus was *Yahweh* in the flesh, who came and died for our sins. In fact, Jesus' main objective in life was to fulfill the meaning of His name by providing salvation through His death, burial, and resurrection. Though *Jesus* was and is a common name today in many lands, He uncommonly fulfilled its meaning!

There is much speculation about who Jesus really was. Some say He was a great prophet. Some say He was a great teacher. Others say He was one of the "ascended masters" or a man who realized His "God consciousness." Some say Christ is a principle of love or good. One day Jesus asked His disciples,

> "Who do people say I am?" They replied, "Some say John the Baptist; others say Elijah; and still others, one of the prophets." "But what about you?" he asked. "Who do you say I am?" Peter answered, "You are the Christ." (Mark 8:27–29)

Christ, or *Christos* in Greek, comes from the Hebrew word *Messiah* meaning "anointed of God." Jesus was the one set apart or anointed by God for the divine purpose of saving humanity. The Old Testament ritual of anointing with oil set persons or objects apart for divine service. Prophets, priests, and kings were anointed with oil. The anointing was to signify God's selection and special empowering for the work to be performed. After the reign of David (1011–971 B.C.), the Hebrews looked forward to the coming of a king from the line of David who would be especially anointed to bring in God's kingdom. This king was given the name *Messiah.* The Messiah would enjoy a special relationship with the Father and be fully empowered for His task (Isaiah 9:1–6; 11:1–5). There was no question in Peter's mind that Jesus was the Christ. Peter witnessed firsthand the life, miracles, and teachings of Jesus and was convinced beyond doubt that Jesus was the Messiah. Therefore, the name Jesus ("God is our Salvation") Christ ("anointed of God") fits our Lord perfectly.

Meditation Time-Out

1. What do Jesus' names tell about His character?
2. What do Jesus' names tell about His work?
3. Who do you say Jesus is?

WONDERFUL COUNSELOR

Read Isaiah 9:6–7

And he will be called Wonderful Counselor . . .

Isaiah 9:6

Coaches such as Dean Smith, Whitey Herzog, and Joe Gibbs have earned the respect of their players because they have proven to be athletically wise. Other coaches pay large sums of money to attend clinics to gain knowledge. But as great as these coaches are, they are human and limited. They are still learning, just like every other coach.

There is only one man who has expertise in all fields and has been proven wise in every situation. His name is Jesus Christ. Another of His names is Wonderful Counselor. Let's look at the characteristics of a good counselor.

First of all, a counselor should be someone who can identify with our need. We read in Hebrews, "For we do not have a high priest who is unable to sympathize with our weaknesses, but we have one who has been tempted in every way, just as we are—yet was without sin" (4:15). Jesus understands our deepest needs even better than we do, because He made us.

Second, a counselor must demonstrate care and compassion. Again we read in Hebrews, "Let us then approach the throne of grace with confidence, so that we may receive mercy and find grace to help us in our time of need" (4:16). The writer exhorts us to approach Him with confidence. Peter says, "Cast all your anxiety on him because he cares for you" (1 Peter 5:7).

Third, a counselor must be available. No human counselor can be available twenty-four hours a day—but Jesus can! We can find grace to help in our time of need, whether it be at 4:00 in the morning or at midday. If we are in the remotest part of the earth, He is there.

Fourth, a counselor must be able to help us through a crisis. Jesus is not only there to help, but He gives the power to overcome. We can receive grace to help in our need. What is *grace?* Grace is God coming to the aid of man. How many counselors perfectly possess all these desirable attributes? Only one. His name is Jesus, and He is truly a wonderful counselor.

⁻ Meditation Time-Out

1. Who predicted Jesus would be a wonderful counselor?
2. What are the traits of a good counselor?
3. How has Jesus been a wonderful counselor to you?

PRINCE OF PEACE

Read Philippians 4:4–13

And he will be called . . .
Prince of Peace.

Isaiah 9:6

P ete Maravich was a living legend, one of the greatest players of basketball, and certainly one of the most colorful. Yet, in spite of all his awards and honors, he was greatly disturbed during his playing days. His team failed to win the championship he longed for, and his critics were never satisfied. Nor did he satisfy himself. He felt responsible for his mother's suicide, his social drinking became a problem, and he had no inner peace. When he retired from basketball, he dabbled in astrology, mysticism, survivalism, nutrition, and UFOs in an attempt to find peace and fulfillment. Once he contemplated suicide while driving his Porsche over a bridge at 140 m.p.h. Then, Pete had a dramatic encounter with Jesus Christ. Late one night in November 1982, as the weight of sin crushed him, Pete rolled out of bed, knelt down, repented of his sin, and put his trust in Jesus Christ. He spoke openly of the emptiness of his former life and the peace and joy Jesus gave him. He had a great effect on many before God took him to heaven in January 1988.

The word *peace* comes from the Hebrew *shalom,* which means "to be quiet, at ease or to enjoy prosperity." One Hebrew greeted another by saying, "Shalom," wishing peace and prosperity to his friend. This peace is more than just the absence of outer conflict; it means contentment of the soul. Only the Prince of Peace can bring rest to a soul. Jesus said, "Peace I leave with you; my peace I give you. I do not give to you as the world gives. Do not let your hearts be troubled and do not be afraid" (John 14:27).

Most of us lack the peace that Pete sought for so long. We are so busy, almost in a frenzy with the demands and pressures of life. We have only one body, but it is pulled in ten different directions. We are filled with fear—fear of the consequences of the past, fear of the present, and fear of an uncertain future. The greatest fear of man is the fear of where he will spend eternity. What will happen when we die? We are afraid to live, yet more afraid to die.

While many people try TM, yoga, or other Eastern religions to find inner peace, Jesus Christ is the only one who can give real, lasting peace to anyone. Though false religions can lower one's heart rate, only the Prince of Peace can put one's heart at ease. Isaiah predicted His role as Prince of Peace (9:6). When He rules our hearts, we have peace with God (Romans 5:1). David experienced this peace (Psalm 27:13), as did Paul while chained inside a Roman prison (Philippians 4). Despite all his successes, Pete Maravich found peace only in Christ. Though the leaders of this world conduct summit meetings and negotiate, peace will only come when the Prince of Peace comes to reign over the earth. Thank God He is coming! Thank God He can reign in our hearts now!

Meditation Time-Out

1. Who is the Prince of Peace?
2. Why will there be no peace until Jesus comes?
3. What is required for Jesus to give peace to your heart?

SON OF DAVID

Read 2 Samuel 7:1–17

Your house and your kingdom will endure forever before me; your throne will be established forever.

2 Samuel 7:16

G reat leaders have the ability to influence men, a charisma that inspires others to follow. The firm but humble direction of coach John Wooten inspired UCLA to great levels in basketball during the 1960s. The intense determination of the Packer's Vince Lombardi inspired the loyalty in his players, which led to their great success. More recently, the exuberant Tommy Lasorda of the Dodgers has led his team to success in the 1980s.

King David had the charisma of a Wooten, a Lombardi, and a Lasorda. But even David didn't compare to the greatest leader ever to walk the earth, the Lord Jesus Christ. As God assured David that the kingdom he established would endure forever, the line of kings of Israel climaxed with Jesus, the last and greatest king of all. Isaiah and Jeremiah recognized this promise to David as a prophecy of the coming Messiah, one who would be the greatest of kings.

> For to us a child is born, to us a son is given, and the government will be on his shoulders. And he will be called Wonderful Counselor, Mighty God, Everlasting Father, Prince of Peace. Of the increase of his government and peace there will be no end. He will reign on David's throne and over his kingdom, establishing and upholding it with justice and righteousness from that time on and forever. The zeal of the LORD Almighty will accomplish this. (Isaiah 9:6–7)

"The days are coming," declares the LORD, "when I will raise up to David a righteous Branch, a King who will reign wisely and do what is just and right in the land." (Jeremiah 23:5)

The Jews understood this prophecy to mean that a king greater than David was coming. He would be a great warrior and would defeat their enemies with the sword. The coming Messiah was to be the Prince of Peace, but the only blood He shed at His first appearance was His own. Therefore, many Jews missed the Messiah when He was on the earth. Their own pride, selfishness, and desire for a great earthly nation blinded them to their king.

The title "Son of David" is confirmed in the New Testament.

- Before Jesus' birth, Zechariah proclaimed that the baby to be born of Mary was to be from the house of David. (Luke 1:69)
- Joseph, the husband of Mary, was from the line of David. (Matthew 1:20)
- A blind man called to "Jesus, Son of David," to heal him. (Mark 10:46–48)
- Peter said that Jesus, the descendant of David, would never suffer decay. (Acts 2:24–36)
- Paul also asserts that Jesus was the Son of David. (Romans 1:3–4; 2 Timothy 2:8)

This title reminds us of His royal blood and of His legal right to kingship. That Jesus is the King of kings is ensured by the fact that He came from a kingly line. Second, this kingly line was to end with Him. While all other kings were merely human, Jesus, being the Son of God, would establish a kingdom that would be over heaven and earth. Therefore, Jesus' earthly subjects are also citizens of heaven (Philippians 3:20). Third, this title was emphasized so that the Jews would not miss Him. Yet, sadly, many did miss Him. Though the Son of David fulfilled prophecy to the letter, they chose to cling to a religious system instead of to the King of kings. Many do the same today. When He appears again, it will be as a mighty warrior who rules His dynasty with a rod of iron.

Meditation Time-Out

1. What distorted perception do people have of Jesus?
2. What does the name "Son of David" say about His person?
3. How will His second coming differ from His first coming?

LAMB OF GOD

Read Isaiah 53

The next day John saw Jesus coming toward him and said, "Look, the Lamb of God, who takes away the sin of the world!"

John 1:29

"T his is for Jim Harris," said Coach Mike Ditka after his 1985 Chicago Bears had defeated the Atlanta Falcons, 36–0. A loyal Bears' fan, Harris was suffering from heart disease at the age of forty-one. The Bears dedicated each play to their dying fan and achieved amazing results in the game.

All mankind was dying of heart disease when God sent His Son to take away our sin. Jesus Christ suffered and died in our place, achieving eternal life for us in the process. As our substitute, He is known as the Lamb of God.

In the Old Testament, a lamb was sacrificed every morning and evening according to the Mosaic law (Exodus 29:38–42). Lambs were used for burnt offerings and sacrifices (Leviticus 9:3; Numbers 15:5). The Passover lamb gives a great picture of what John the Baptist recognized when he called Jesus the "Lamb of God." The lamb had to meet certain requirements. First, it had to be perfect, without blemish of any kind (Exodus 12:5). Second, the lamb was to be a year-old male, in its prime of life, healthy and strong—a picture of Jesus who was slain on the cross in His prime, age thirty-three.

Third, the lamb was to be taken into the house for four days and then killed (Exodus 12:3–6). The emotional pain each home would feel when they killed the lamb they had grown to love would remind Israel of the terrible cost of sin. Fourth, the blood on the doorposts that saved everyone inside the house pictured the violent death of Christ, which saves us from God's wrath.

Lambs are gentle animals who are generally submissive. Isaiah prophesied Jesus' sufferings: "He was led like a lamb to the slaughter, and as a sheep before her shearers is silent, so he did not open his mouth" (Isaiah 53:7). Peter wrote, "When they hurled their insults at him, he did not retaliate; when he suffered, he made no threats. Instead, he entrusted himself to him who judges justly" (1 Peter 2:23).

In Revelation 5 is one final scene of Jesus as the Lamb of God. The Lamb, looking as if it had been slain, stood in the center of the throne of heaven and received the worship of all heavenly creatures (vv. 6–14). He alone was found worthy to open the sealed judgments of God's scroll. He alone is worthy to judge the earth. "Worthy is the Lamb, who was slain, to receive power and wealth and wisdom and strength and honor and glory and praise!" (Revelation 5:12).

Meditation Time-Out

1. How was Jesus like a lamb?
2. How did the Old Testament sacrifices picture Jesus' death?
3. What did Jesus' death accomplish?

PART 3

THE CHAMPION OF OUR SALVATION

The King Who Conquered Through Death

. . . so that by his death he might destroy him who holds the power of death—that is, the devil—and free those who all their lives were held in slavery by their fear of death.

Hebrews 2:14–15

HIS DEATH

Read Matthew 16:21–28

From that time on Jesus began to explain to his disciples that he must go to Jerusalem and suffer many things at the hands of the elders, chief priests and teachers of the law, and that he must be killed and on the third day be raised to life.

Matthew 16:21

A s owner of the L. A. Raiders, Al Davis has long held the reputa- tion of a man who dominates both people and circumstances. He has been a "get it done" type of person, one who refuses to let obstacles deter him. But recently, Davis has faced the reality of an obstacle that scares him. "Death is the only thing I'm afraid of," he told ESPN's Pete Axthelm in the spring of 1989. "It's the one thing you can't control."

Al Davis is right. He has no control over death. Nor has any other man. But Jesus Christ, the God-Man, is the master of life *and* death. He came to earth to die and be raised by His Father so that God's righteous requirements for sinful man to come to Himself might be met for all who trust Jesus. He died in our place so that we might know God.

Jesus' death is the focal point of Scripture.

- Paul says it is of *first* importance. (1 Corinthians 15:3)
- Jesus expressly outlined His suffering to the disciples. (Matthew 16:21)
- He said that He would be killed to provide eternal life to whoever believed in Him. (John 3:14–16)
- He sovereignly engineered His death in fulfillment of prophecy. (Luke 9:28–31)

69

- Though the prophets spoke of His suffering, they didn't fully understand it. Even angels long to examine the magnitude of His plan. (1 Peter 1:10–12)
- Jesus' death is the theme of songs in heaven. (Revelation 5:8–10)
- It is proclaimed on earth when believers drink the wine and eat the bread of communion. (1 Corinthians 11:26)
- While we are saved by faith in Christ alone, we outwardly identify with Him through baptism. (Romans 6:3)
- His death ransomed us from the clutches of sin. (Matthew 20:28)
- Jesus Christ is the only way to God, and His death is the means of approaching God. (John 14:6)
- He paid for our sins once for all time, and His death will never be repeated. (1 Peter 3:18)
- His sacrifice is finished, complete, and eternal. (Hebrews 9:25–28; 10:12)
- The death of Jesus Christ made salvation possible for all men of all ages. (2 Corinthians 5:14–15; Hebrews 2:9)
- Salvation and all His blessings are given only to believers. (John 3:17–18)

Our Lord Jesus had no fear of death. Jesus holds the key to death and hell (Revelation 1:18). His death provides our salvation, and His resurrection proves His authority.

Meditation Time-Out

1. What is the meaning of Jesus' death?
2. What do communion and baptism have to do with the death of Jesus?
3. Who benefits from the death of Jesus?

HIS RESURRECTION

Read 1 Corinthians 15

God raised him from the dead, freeing him from the agony of death, because it was impossible for death to keep its hold on him.

Acts 2:24

The football I'll get straight," says Al Davis. "My biggest thing now is this death business. I've always been able to control the elements of my life, dominate my environment without hurting others. But this death business—I can't beat it. I can't win."

Like Al Davis, many people are worried about their appointment with this thing called death. But there is one man who tasted death for every man and overcame it! The greatest fact of history is that Jesus Christ arose from the dead! After suffering death and being raised to life, He appeared many times over a forty-day period to prove Himself conqueror of our greatest enemy (Acts 1:3). The Jewish religious leaders could not produce His dead body and deny the claims of His resurrection. It was hard to produce a corpse when the living, risen Lord Jesus was right in front of them! Many eyewitnesses spoke of this fact (Acts 2:32).

Belief in His resurrection remains essential to salvation today (Romans 10:9–10). The resurrection of Jesus Christ is the foundation of Christianity (1 Corinthians 15:1–4). The Old Testament predicts His resurrection, and over one hundred New Testament scriptures confirm it. Jesus says that He was dead, is now alive forever, and holds the keys of death and Hades (Revelation 1:10).

The resurrection of Jesus Christ gives us a solid basis for our faith. We know that He is trustworthy and that God is faithful because Jesus lives (1 Peter 1:21). Because He arose, we know He is indeed God (Romans 1:4). We are assured His sacrifice for our sins was accepted by God, and we are justified because He arose (Romans 4:25). Our eternal salvation is secure because He lives (Romans 10:9–10). We have a living high priest interceding for us constantly before the Father (Romans 8:34). He lives to plead our case (Hebrews 7:25). He is our defender, speaking to God on the basis of His sacrifice (1 John 2:1–2).

Because God raised Jesus from the dead, He will also resurrect us (2 Corinthians 4:14; 1 Thessalonians 4:14). Because He lives, we will live also (John 14:19). What a promise! We no longer fear death. In Jesus, we have victory over man's greatest foe.

Meditation Time-Out

1. Who tasted death for every man?
2. How do you know Jesus is alive?
3. What does the Resurrection mean to you?

HIS RETURN TO HEAVEN

Read Acts 1:1–11

He was taken up before their very eyes, and a cloud hid him from their sight.

Acts 1:9

Many individual champions and even entire teams have been invited by the president to special celebrations at the White House. These occasions cannot occur the same day the championship is won; they are delayed until preparations are completed. The attention of the nation, even the world, is directed toward the winners. The knowledge of their success is spread far and wide by such exposure.

Christ's visible departure from earth to heaven meant much more for the world than any trip to the White House. Jesus predicted His ascension when He said, "I go to the one who sent me" (John 7:33). He said He was "going to the Father" (John 14:28). Mark 16:19 tells us that He was taken up to heaven. Luke 24:50–51 says that the Ascension occurred as Jesus was blessing His disciples. Acts 1:9 tells us that He was taken from before their very eyes and a cloud hid Him from their sight. Stephen saw Him in heaven as he was being stoned (Acts 7:55–56). Peter said He is exalted to the right hand of God (Acts 2:33; 5:31; 1 Peter 3:22). Paul saw a light from heaven and heard Jesus call to him (Acts 9:3–5; 22:6–8; 26:13–15). John saw the Lamb of God in heaven (Revelation 5:6–14).

Jesus' ascension is part of the mystery of godliness (1 Timothy 3:16). We don't understand every facet of His exaltation, but we do know several results.

- He is now highly exalted and has a name above every name. (Philippians 2:9)

- He is our High Priest, interceding before God's throne for us. (Hebrews 7:25)
- He is preparing our future home. (John 14:1–4)
- He has led captivity captive and given us gifts so we can do His work. (Ephesians 4:7–12)
- He will one day return from heaven as Lord and King over the earth. (1 Thessalonians 4:13–18)

After winning His "championship" over sin on the cross, our Lord Jesus ascended to the Father (John 14:28–29). He makes all who are in Christ into eternal winners, destined to be with Him someday. Like today's athletic champion, our celebration in glory is delayed while He makes final preparations. He will return in the same way He left (Acts 1:11). Because He went to heaven, the Comforter came to indwell us (John 16:5–7). Our minds should be set on heaven, the home of Him who is our life (Colossians 3:1–3).

Meditation Time-Out

1. What was Jesus doing when He ascended?
2. Who saw Him ascend to heaven?
3. What is Jesus doing now that He is in heaven?

HIS PRESENT WORK

Read Hebrews 7

*Who is he that condemns?
Christ Jesus, who died—more
than that, who was raised to
life—is at the right hand of God
and is also interceding for us.*

Romans 8:34

H uman officials are imperfect. They make mistakes in judgment and sometimes in the application of the rules of a game. At such times, a good coach must intercede on behalf of his players. This should be done tactfully and without loss of self-control, but it must be done. While a protest may not change a call, it encourages players to know they have a coach who will intercede on their behalf when they have a legitimate complaint.

The Christian has an intercessor before God in the courts of heaven. His name is Jesus Christ. The Bible says, "He is able to save completely those who come to God through him, because he always lives to intercede for them" (Hebrews 7:25). He entered heaven to appear before God for us (Hebrews 9:24). He is always pleading our case. Satan's accusations are countered by Jesus' arguments (Revelation 12:10). When we sin—and all of us sin every day in some way—Jesus speaks to the Father on the basis of His sacrifice in payment for us (1 John 2:1–2). That's why the saved man can never be lost. Jesus saved us, and now He keeps us saved by continually pleading on the basis of His shed blood. If our plea were on any other basis, we would be lost. But God always hears Jesus' prayers (John 11:41) and always answers yes to Him because Jesus always prays in line with God's perfect will. Our salvation is eternally secure because He is eternally on the job, interceding for His team.

What assurance to know that Jesus is on our side. We have a head coach who knows all about us, who cares for us, and who represents us before God. He perfectly pleads our cause, and He has never yet lost a case.

Meditation Time-Out

1. What does Jesus answer to Satan's accusations?
2. How does Jesus' intercession for you make you feel?
3. Why does God always say yes to Jesus' prayers?

HIS MESSAGE TO HIS TEAM

Read Revelation 1–3

Write, therefore, what you have seen, what is now and what will take place later.

Revelation 1:19

Halftime is when thousands of fans buy snacks, sip soft drinks, and visit the rest rooms. But for those who play the game, it is a time to be rebriefed, encouraged, and challenged by the head coach to finish the game with a determined effort. Every good coach describes what is strategically necessary to win, and the team is responsible to go back into action and implement his instructions.

Our Lord Jesus gave a great "halftime speech" to His churches in chapters 2 and 3 of Revelation. He appeared in majestic glory to John, who was exiled to Patmos because of his testimony about Christ (Revelation 1:9). Suddenly, Jesus appeared with a message to the seven churches of Asia Minor. These messages apply to seven types of churches and to individual Christians even today.

How does John describe Jesus' appearance (Revelation 1:12-16)? The robe reaching to His feet spoke of His authority. His head and hair were white like wool, as white as snow, which spoke of His purity. His eyes were like blazing fire, able to penetrate and expose sin. His feet were like bronze glowing in a furnace, able to tread upon evil. His voice was like the sound of rushing waters—urgent, demanding, and imperative. He had a sharp double-edged sword in His mouth, indicative of the piercing, penetrating Word of God. His face was like the sun—glorious!

John's only response was to fall at His feet as though dead (Revelation 1:17). Then Jesus delivered His word and commanded John to write it down. Jesus had words of both encouragement and discipline. In the

Ephesian message, He chastised those who were doctrinally sound but had lost that intense first love for Him. In His message to Smyrna, He encouraged those who suffered. He praised their faithfulness, but condemned the false religiosity of the group at Pergaman, the center of satanic power. He blasted the false teaching of Thyatira and the spiritual deadness of Sardis. He had words of comfort and encouragement for those who faithfully lived by His Word in Philadelphia, but He rebuked the lukewarm church at Laodicea.

Sometimes we who are on God's team need discipline, and sometimes we need encouragement. Often we need both. Jesus Christ is our great master coach, able to give the best halftime talks. After a session with Him, we cannot help but win the second half!

Meditation Time-Out

1. How did Jesus appear to John?
2. Why did Jesus appear to John?
3. What would Jesus say to you?

CATCHING AWAY HIS TEAM

Read 1 Thessalonians 4:13–18

For the Lord himself will come down from heaven, with a loud command, with the voice of the archangel and with the trumpet call of God, and the dead in Christ will rise first. After that, we who are still alive and are left will be caught up together with them in the clouds to meet the Lord in the air. And so we will be with the Lord forever.

1 Thessalonians 4:16–17

The pro draft is a tense and exciting time for college athletes. Many wait anxiously as the teams pick their prospects. To be selected is a great honor and usually brings great financial reward. Players anticipate bright futures, knowing they are wanted by the organization which chooses them.

The Lord Jesus has both selected and signed all believers in Himself. He chose us "before the creation of the world" (Ephesians 1:4) and "signed us" forever on the day we trusted Him as Savior. He has never lost one of His recruits. One day, He will return to catch us away in dramatic fashion. At some point in the future—maybe very soon—Jesus Christ will interrupt history with His personal, bodily appearance. He will bring the souls of those who have died in Christ, resurrect their bodies, and "catch up" those living believers to meet Him in the clouds. It will be a great reunion with believers who have died, but an even greater thrill to see the Lord Jesus for the first time.

What do we know about this "body snatching"? We know we will be gathered to Him (2 Thessalonians 2:1). Our blessed hope is His glorious appearing (Titus 2:13). We will be rescued from God's coming wrath (1 Thessalonians 1:10; 5:9). There will be a loud command, the voice of the archangel, and the trumpet call of God (1 Thessalonians 4:16). The Christian dead will be raised, and then the living believers will be caught up in the clouds to meet Jesus (1 Thessalonians 4:17). Jesus will transform our bodies to be like His glorious body (Philippians 3:21). This occurs in the "twinkling of an eye" (1 Corinthians 15:50–54). The General Electric company says that the "twinkling of an eye" is $11/100$ of a second. It's only enough time to open your eyes after having closed them. One second we are on earth, the next we are with Jesus in the air—forever.

No man knows the date of this "catching away" of God's team. We know it is a certainty because God promised to do it. The question is: Are you a believer in Jesus Christ? If so, you will take part in a great victory celebration.

Meditation Time-Out

1. What do you know about Jesus' return?
2. How can you be ready for His return?
3. How long will Christians be with the Lord?

OUR KING

Read Revelation 20:1–10

I [God] have installed my King [Jesus] on Zion, my holy hill. . . . You [the King] will rule them [the nations] with an iron scepter. . . . Therefore, you kings, be wise; be warned, you rulers of the earth. . . . Kiss the Son, lest he be angry and you be destroyed in your way.

Psalm 2:6, 9, 10, 12

How ironic are events in the world of sports. For example, one of baseball's all-time greats, Robin Roberts, allowed more home runs (501) than anyone else in his career. And the great Connie Mack, renowned as a strategic genius, never won a pennant in forty-four years as manager. One could certainly not predict those statistics.

There are many unpredictable juxtapositions about God's kingdom given in Scripture. Old Testament scriptures speak of a suffering servant who would be a meek and lowly messiah, while at the same time mentioning a conquering king who would rule the world. Many Jewish leaders thought there would be two messiahs. They rejected Jesus because He didn't set up a visible kingdom on earth and bring an end to Roman tyranny.

Looking back, we see what they didn't see: that the coming of Christ to redeem mankind was in two phases. He came first as a suffering servant to die for our sins, making it possible for us to fellowship with God. At the Second Coming, Christ will come as King and will set up His kingdom on earth and reign for one thousand years. He will physically restore the dominion of good over evil on this planet. Satan will be bound in the abyss for one thousand years, let loose for a brief time to deceive those who have rejected the Lord personally, recaptured, and thrown into the lake of burning sulfur to be tormented day and night forever and ever.

- The government will be upon Jesus' shoulders. (Isaiah 9:6)
- There will be no end to the increase of His government and peace. (Isaiah 9:7)
- He will rule with a rod of iron. (Revelation 19:15)
- He will judge righteously and will slay the wicked. (Isaiah 11:3–5)
- Nature's law of tooth and claw will be changed, as the effects of sin are removed. Animals will no longer be carnivorous. (Isaiah 11:6–8)
- The knowledge of the Lord will cover the earth. (Isaiah 11:9)

Jesus Christ is the rightful ruler of this earth. When He returns, the kingdom of the world will become the Kingdom of our Lord and of His Christ, and He will reign forever and ever (Revelation 11:15). We request this rule every time we pray, "Your kingdom come, your will be done on earth as it is in heaven" (Matthew 6:10). The principles Jesus taught in the Sermon on the Mount (Matthew 5–7) will be lived universally. What a great day that will be.

Meditation Time-Out

1. How will Jesus' rule change the earth?
2. Where is Satan when Jesus rules the world?
3. How is a relationship with God established?

THE JUDGE

Read Revelation 20:11–15

For he has set a day when he will judge the world with justice by the man he has appointed. He has given proof of this to all men by raising him from the dead.

Acts 17:31

In the 1948 World Series opener, Bob Feller of the Indians signaled shortstop Lou Boudreau for a pickoff play in the eighth inning of a 0–0 game. The Braves' Phil Masi dove headfirst back into second, seemingly a "dead duck." But umpire Billy Stewart called him safe amid howls of protest. Moments later, Tommy Holmes singled home the game's only run, and Feller lost a two-hitter! The questionable judgment of a human umpire cost a great pitcher a key World Series' game.

Because God is holy, He must judge sin. Because He is righteous (unlike human umpires), His judgment is always right. Judgment by Jesus Christ is one of the most certain events of the future. All of us instinctively know it is true, for it is imprinted in our hearts. God's throne is established for judgment, and He will judge the world with justice by the man He has appointed (Acts 17:31). That man is Jesus Himself (John 5:22).

Our Lord Jesus is uniquely qualified to judge the world. As the sinless Son of God, He took upon Himself our sins and was judged by God the Father in our place. The Cross was the great judgment of God against sin. As judge, God has correctly proclaimed all of us guilty of sin. He then stepped down from the judgment bench, became man, and died in our place. He did not come to condemn us (we were already condemned) but to save us (John 3:17–18). When we trust Jesus' sacrifice for us, we are saved. When Jesus returns, He will judge His people at His judgment seat according to what we have done (2 Corinthians 5:10; Revelation 22:12). Remember, we are not talking about whether believers in Jesus are saved to heaven or lost in hell. We are saved *immediately* and *eternally* the moment we trust Christ to save us. How will God judge us?

- Salvation is free with no strings attached, for God didn't save us to place us on probation. But the degree of rewards in heaven is determined by our works. (Matthew 16:27)
- Our motives will be exposed. (1 Corinthians 4:5)
- Our use of talents (Luke 19), opportunities (Matthew 20), and the quality of our works (1 Corinthians 3:11–15) will be examined.
- We will be rewarded for winning souls to Christ (1 Thessalonians 2:19), for faithful stewardship of His resources (Matthew 25:14–30), for good deeds (Matthew 10:40–42; 25:34–46), and for suffering for Christ. (Matthew 5:10–12; Luke 6:22–23)

The rewards given are crowns:

- crowns of life (James 1:12);
- crowns of glory (1 Peter 5:4);
- crowns of righteousness (2 Timothy 4:7–8);
- crowns of rejoicing (1 Thessalonians 2:10–20);
- and an incorruptible crown for self-discipline. (1 Corinthians 9:25–27)

We must be faithful and alert, for the rewards we may have enjoyed can still be lost through unwise investment of time, talent, and treasure (1 Corinthians 3:15; 2 John 8).

God's Word speaks of several other judgments, all executed by the Lord Jesus Christ. He will judge Israel with a great tribulation (Psalm 50; Malachi 3). He will judge the Gentile nations (Matthew 25:31–32; Zechariah 14), Satan and fallen angels (Revelation 20:1–10), and all unbelieving men at His great white throne (Revelation 20:11–15).

Meditation Time-Out

1. What rewards are given to God's people for faithfulness?
2. What punishment is given to unbelievers at the Great White Throne?

FOREVER THE WINNER

Read Revelation 19

On his robe and on his thigh he has this name written: KING OF KINGS AND LORD OF LORDS.

Revelation 19:16

M any coaches and writers called Indiana State a team of destiny during Larry Bird's senior year. New Mexico State Coach Ken Hayes was one of them, as his team lost three times to the Sycamores. "When you're ahead by two points with three seconds to play and are shooting a foul shot (there were no three-point baskets in those days), you've got to feel comfortable," Hayes said of a February game against ISU. But NMSU missed the free throw and the rebound, and Bob Heaton hit a forty-five-foot "buzzer beater" to tie the game.

"This type of thing happens once in a hundred years," Hayes said, as ISU won 91–89 in overtime.

ISU may or may not have been a team of destiny, but we know a man who was a man of destiny. His name is Jesus Christ. Though the struggle was fierce, Jesus overcame every obstacle. Our Lord Jesus endured great temptation; He was proved perfect. He was tortured beyond imagination and forsaken by a loving Father. He died for our sins, the just for the unjust, but God raised Him from the dead. The grave could not hold Him. He ascended to heaven and led captivity captive. He sits on the throne of the universe.

Jesus is Lord. Satan is not a sovereign lord. Circumstances are not king. Puny men have no power before Christ. The faithful and true One, followed by the armies of heaven, will one day return to the earth to rule as King of kings and Lord of lords (Revelation 19:11–16).

Because He wins, we win. We are completely identified with Him the moment we trust Him to save us. This means we identify with His death by dying to selfishness. We identify with His resurrection in the new life He gives us. We identify with His ascension to heaven when we physically die. To be absent from this body is to be present with the Lord Himself (2 Corinthians 5:8). We have an inheritance in heaven reserved for us that can never perish, spoil or fade away (1 Peter 1:3–5). We will be with King Jesus forever (1 Thessalonians 4:16–17). Faith and love spring from this sure hope (Colossians 1:5). We have reason to celebrate. We can smile in adversity because we are on the winning team. We have a great Savior, and He can never fail us.

Meditation Time-Out

1. Who destined Jesus for rulership of the earth?
2. What will Jesus look like when He appears?
3. How are we identified with Jesus?

GAME PLAN OF GOD'S MAN

An Athlete's Guide Through John's Gospel

For God so loved the world that he gave his one and only Son, that whoever believes in him shall not perish but have eternal life.

John 3:16

THE WORD BECAME FLESH

Read John 1:1–14

*In the beginning was the Word.
. . . The Word became flesh and
made his dwelling among us.*

John 1:1, 14

A coach who can demonstrate the fundamentals of a physical skill is superior to one who only tells a player how to play a position. That is one reason why many of today's successful mentors have had a comprehensive background of playing the game themselves. Their words become more meaningful when backed by experience and a certain degree of skill.

The scripture teaches that the Word, Jesus Christ, existed from eternity, was equal with God the Father, and created everything (1:1–3). Moreover, life itself was in Him (v. 4). But if the Son of God had remained in heaven with the Father, we would not have known God's grace and truth, nor would we have been able to believe in Him and be saved out of the terrible darkness of sin. It is mind-boggling to think that God Himself would leave heaven, take on the form of man, and "pitch His tent" on this earth for thirty-three years. The angels must have been dumbfounded when the announcement of God's plan was made. How they praised God on the night the Savior was born in Bethlehem almost two thousand years ago. A visual demonstration of God's great love and forgiveness was all wrapped up in the person of Christ. As the eternal Creator, He alone is qualified as "Master Coach" of the universe.

Today's athlete often asks "why?" The answer is that we might receive Him as personal Savior by believing on His name. The example of His perfect life makes His words all the more believable. He died not for His own sins, but for ours. Then He was raised for our justification

(Romans 4:25), that we might be declared righteous before God. Do you believe Him? If so, you are an adopted child of God (John 1:12), destined to spend eternity in His presence.

Meditation Time-Out

1. Who was the Word?
2. How long has the Word been in existence?
3. Why did the Word come into the world?

VOICE IN THE DESERT

Read John 1:14–34

This was he [Jesus] of whom I [John the Baptist] said, "He who comes after me has surpassed me because he was before me."

John 1:15

I t is the duty of a sports information director to publish reports of the merits and achievements of others. No worthy sports reporter draws attention to himself by printing his credentials. His total focus is on those who score the touchdowns, make the free throws, or hit the home runs.

John the Baptist, though not the writer of the book of John, would have made an excellent sports reporter. Because of his call from God, he unashamedly took a back seat to the Lord Jesus and directed all the attention of the people to Him. When asked directly who he was, John replied simply, "I am the voice . . ." (v. 23). He claimed to be no more than just a voice to direct the attention of others to God in the flesh. And he certainly had big news to declare. Though no one had ever seen God, Jesus was now making Him known to man (v. 18). He was the Lamb of God who came to take away the sin of the world (v. 29). He came that He might empower us with God's Spirit (v. 33). No reporter has ever had a bigger scoop than John the Baptist.

Some athletes love to draw attention to themselves. They talk about their achievements, their awards, and their ability. But like John, a Christian must direct attention to the One who has all the credentials, the only truly worthy One—Jesus Christ. We only find true joy and fulfillment in giving glory to Him.

Meditation Time-Out

1. According to the Jews, who was John the Baptist?
2. Why was Jesus called "the Lamb of God"?
3. How did John know Jesus was God's Son?

CHOOSING HIS TEAM

Read John 1:35–50

"I saw you while you were still under the fig tree before Philip called you."

John 1:48

R emember as a sandlot player how two captains would choose up sides to play a ball game? You were tense with expectation until your name was called and joyfully relieved when someone chose you. The captains usually knew everyone's abilities and chose on that basis; a new boy on the block was a real risk. No one knew how good he could play until the game began.

Our Master Coach has infinitely more knowledge than any earthly team captain. As He chose His team of disciples, He knew every detail of their background. Nathanael was amazed to find out that Jesus not only knew that he was an honest man, but He also knew where he had been (under a fig tree) and what he was doing (meditating) when Philip told him about finding the Messiah. Perhaps Nathanael was thinking of Jacob's dream and the angels he had seen going from heaven to earth on a ladder (Genesis 28:12). Jesus now proclaimed that He would replace the ladder as God's link to earth and that man could now communicate with God through Him. What a claim! No wonder Nathanael believed and followed Him.

Jesus Christ knows every detail of your life, too (Psalm 139). He knows your physical position, your every thought, every habit, every word, where you live, your physical stature, and your every desire. In His omniscience, He sovereignly chooses those who follow Him (John 15:16). All this is incomprehensible to us. The only logical response to such an all-knowing God is to follow Him with determined love.

Meditation Time-Out

1. Did Nazareth, Jesus' home, have a good reputation?
2. What caused Nathanael to trust in Jesus?
3. By what title did Jesus refer to Himself?

TASTE OF NEW WINE

Read John 2:1–11

This, the first of his miraculous signs, Jesus performed at Cana in Galilee. He thus revealed his glory, and his disciples put their faith in him.

John 2:11

For many athletes and coaches, advancing from one level of play to another is a goal which brings much satisfaction. A college player is elated to sign that first contract and enter professional baseball. A minor leaguer who goes to the big leagues considers it the fulfillment of a dream. It is very hard for one who has played or coached at a higher level to be sent back down to a lower classification. Things never seem the same on the smaller scale.

The first miracle Jesus performed while on earth was the changing of water into wine at the Cana wedding feast. By this sign, the Lord began to draw attention to who He was. When the banquet master tasted the new wine, he recognized that it was far superior to the old wine which had first been consumed. Jesus was demonstrating that the new covenant was an improvement over the old; God had kept His best, Jesus Christ, until now. How futile and senseless it would be to ever think about going back to the old covenant system. Now that the Messiah was here, things would never be the same.

Notice the responses of those at the banquet. The banquet master was ignorant of the work. Though he complimented the bridegroom, he didn't recognize the miracle. And the servants who had drawn the water only had a head knowledge of the source of the new wine. Only the disciples were moved by the miracle to put their faith in Him (v. 11).

Does Jesus' person and work move you to trust Him? Or do you only have a head knowledge of Him? Why dwell in the minor leagues of a religious system when you can know Christ personally and enjoy life on a higher plane?

Meditation Time-Out

1. Why did Jesus perform this miracle?
2. What does changing water into wine tell you about His sharing in human joys?
3. How did this miracle reveal His glory?

RELIGION MADE EASY

Read John 2:12–25

*"How dare you turn my
Father's house into a market!"*

John 2:16

S ome athletes are always looking for ways to do a difficult job without making the sacrifices and doing the hard work necessary for success. Sometimes, because of being pampered from childhood, many players seek the easy way out and never realize their potential. In fact, there is no easy way to attain the physical condition necessary for excellence. Only much study and sweat enables a competitor to reach his potential. Those who try to avoid the pain never realize the gain.

When Jesus was on earth, the corrupt Jewish religious leaders were attempting to make religion easy for Israel. During Passover, blood sacrifices were required by Old Testament law, and the Jews set up a thriving business inside the temple area. This magnificent marble and gold structure, surrounded by four courtyards and measuring one thousand feet on each side, covered approximately four city blocks. Jewish travelers from all over the world found it convenient to purchase (at inflated prices) a sacrifice to fulfill their religious duty. They also exchanged currency (and were ripped off in the process) to pay the temple tax. Therefore, they conveniently felt absolved of religious obligation, while the Jewish religious leaders profited.

On two occasions, Jesus' moral indignation led Him to drive out the merchants and money changers. This first time He caught them by surprise. The second cleansing of the temple was just before His arrest. In standing for righteous use of His Father's house, He defied the religious establishment. The basis of His authority was His relationship to God. He derived authority by being in submission to His Father. Notice that

Jesus never forced anyone into the temple, but He did use force to drive out those who profaned it.

True righteousness is never cheap. It is based upon right standing with God and it cost Jesus His life. Are you using good works to attain righteousness? His righteousness alone is sufficient. Rest in that sufficiency today.

Meditation Time-Out

1. How do men try to take advantage of Christianity?
2. When have you been morally indignant?
3. How does the world react to those who speak out against sin?

A BRAND NEW LIFE

Read John 3:1–21

"I tell you the truth, no one can see the kingdom of God unless he is born again.

John 3:3

Most people have a general understanding of the familiar phrase "born again." A team hopelessly behind late in the game receives renewed inspiration and makes a late comeback to win the game. A player thought to be well "over the hill" in his career makes some adjustments in his game, and his success is restored. A franchise acquires new players, changes marketing techniques, and enjoys prosperity as a result. Such drastic changes are often labeled "born-again" situations.

But what did Jesus mean when He told a well-respected religious leader of the Jews, "You must be born again [from above]"? The man, Nicodemus, had come to talk to the Lord personally and privately one night to find out Jesus' real identity. Not only did he discover who Jesus was, but he also discovered something about himself. Like all of us, Nicodemus was born with a sinful nature inclined continually toward evil (Genesis 6:5) and could never please God (Romans 8:7–8). Naturally, apart from Christ we can never understand the things of God (1 Corinthians 2:14), and therefore can never see God (Hebrews 12:14).

But supernaturally, we can be "born from above!" Paul wrote, "Therefore, if any one is in Christ, he is a new creation" (2 Corinthians 5:17). This spiritual rebirth takes place when we simply look to Jesus as the Israelites looked to the uplifted serpent in the wilderness (Numbers 21:4-9).

John makes it clear that God loves us and desires to save us (John 3:16). It is equally clear that we are naturally under condemnation because of our sin and our failure to trust Christ (v. 18). Men naturally love darkness because it hides their sin (v. 19). But the good news is that if we will turn to Christ, He will forgive our sin and give us everlasting life. Why not trust Christ for the greatest comeback ever and receive eternal life by being born again by His Spirit?

Meditation Time-Out

1. Why must we be born again?
2. Why did God send His Son into the world?
3. What happens to those who do not trust God's Son?

A CERTAIN OUTCOME

Read John 3:22–36

Whoever believes in the Son has eternal life, but whoever rejects the Son will not see life, for God's wrath remains on him.

John 3:36

M any things in athletics are tentative and uncertain. It is possible for a team to be well prepared for a game and still lose. Or sometimes a player will make a mistake which works out to the benefit of his team. For example, in the 1984 Kansas High School All-Star baseball game, a hitter for the East team missed a squeeze bunt attempt, and the runner from third was caught in a rundown. However, the catcher threw the ball away, and two decisive runs were scored!

There is no uncertainty about the truth as explained in John 3:36, however. Because of sin in man, apart from Jesus Christ he is hopelessly and eternally lost. A man who rejects God's only provision for sin either by active rebellion or passive indifference is not only separated from God now but will suffer the consequences of sin for all eternity. The wrath of God, His righteous response to sin, is upon such a person and remains on him forever.

But whoever believes in Jesus Christ and trusts Him as his only hope of salvation has eternal life now. Such a person has admitted his sin to the Father, been willing to leave it, and accepted the death of Christ on the cross on his behalf. He has passed from death to life and is as assured of heaven as if he were already there. All this occurs by the grace of God through faith on the part of the believer. With such a certain outcome it only makes sense to trust Christ, doesn't it?

Meditation Time-Out

1. Did John the Baptist exalt himself or someone else?
2. When does eternal life begin?
3. What is the condition of people who reject Christ now?

THE WELL
OF LIVING WATER

Read John 4:1–26

*"Everyone who drinks this
water will be thirsty again, but
whoever drinks the water I give
him will never thirst."*

John 4:13–14

O ne of the cliches in athletics is that success breeds success. In
other words, winning can become a habit, almost a necessity. In
fact, the more a team wins, the more it expects to win and the more the
public expects it to win. Many highly successful football programs like
those in Texas, Nebraska, or Alabama consider it a bad year and experience frustration if they are not ranked number one at the season's end.
Obviously, simply winning games, along with the money and recognition that comes with it, is not permanently satisfying.

Though the cup of materialism, temporal success, and recognition
offered by the world leaves man's thirst momentarily quenched, the living water Jesus offers us—eternal life through His Spirit—totally and
permanently satisfies. Nowhere did Jesus teach this principle more
clearly than at Jacob's well, in those days one of the deepest in Palestine—eighty-five feet. A Samaritan woman came alone in the heat of the
day to find water, and as if by divine appointment, Jesus was there wait-
ing. He offered her "living water," revealed supernatural knowledge of
her past, and gently allowed the Spirit to point out her need of Him.
When she tried to divert the conversation to religious differences (places
of worship), Jesus pointed out that the place of worship doesn't matter.
He said that worship in spirit (with the right attitude) and in truth (based

upon the right information about God) is what counts. Then He clearly revealed Himself as the Messiah.

At which well are you drinking today? The thrill of winning games, making money, or earning the recognition of others is fleeting and will eventually leave you thirsty again. But if you drink the living water offered by Jesus, you will enjoy permanent satisfaction in knowing forgiveness of sin and the peace of knowing you have eternal life.

Meditation Time-Out

1. Does winning games give lasting satisfaction?
2. Why did a busy Jesus take time to talk to one person?
3. What does worship have to do with serving Christ?

MEAT AND GOD'S WILL

Read John 4:27–42

"My food," said Jesus, "is to do the will of him who sent me and to finish his work."

John 4:34

Many ballplayers have had the same experience as one college outfielder from Eastern Michigan who related, "As kids, we played baseball from right after breakfast until dusk in one of the neighbor yards. Every day we rotated to a different yard, and our play was only interrupted by a call for lunch. The mother of the 'home yard' fed us, but we only stopped for a short ten minutes because we had to. Then we were back to the game. We only went home because it got too dark to play." These kids were obviously more excited about playing baseball than they were about eating or sleeping.

Doing the Father's will was always more important to Jesus than eating or sleeping. When the disciples left Him at the well, He was tired, thirsty, and probably hungry. When they returned with food, His concern for feeding hungry hearts overshadowed His physical needs. The will of the Father motivated His life.

Meeting the needs of people by feeding them the "Bread of Life" should be a compelling force in our lives, too. Rather than catering to our materialistic desires for things, our appetite for entertainment, or even legitimate needs for food and sleep, we must find fulfillment in meeting the needs of others by sharing God's Word with them. We need to be concerned about doing His will instead of ours. The fields of people are still as ready for harvest as they were two thousand years ago. Some sow the seed, others water it, and still others harvest souls for Christ, but all have a part. A Christian's role may differ at times, or he may be involved in all three phases. The important thing is setting your mind to do the will of the Father, who constantly seeks to save lost men and is not willing that any should perish (2 Peter 3:9).

Meditation Time-Out

1. How have you "fed" others?
2. What does your mindset have to do with John 4:34?
3. What gives you the most fulfillment in life?

NOT DISCOURAGED BY DISTANCE

Read John 4:43–54

Jesus replied, "You may go. Your son will live." The man took Jesus at his word and departed.

John 4:50

B ob Wieland is not a man to be discouraged by distance. As a combat medic in Vietnam, Bob lost both legs in a Vietcong booby trap in June 1969. In only six weeks, he was totally independent; normal recovery time is up to one and one-half years. He proceeded to set weight-lifting records while lifting against able-bodied men. For six years he served as a physical education instructor at Cal State University, Los Angeles. In 1982, Bob set out on a 2,770-mile walk across America—on his hands!

The government official who came to Jesus in Galilee must not have been discouraged by distance either. He came in desperate need and asked for mercy for his son. Neither money nor position could meet the need in his life. So he walked the twenty to twenty-five miles from Capernaum to Cana, hoping that Jesus would save the boy's life. He did not come to argue with the Master or demand a sign of Jesus' deity like so many of the Jews. All he sought was mercy.

Jesus blessed that attitude. He healed the boy, and the man departed for home by faith. Though a good distance from the child, the power of God was just as evident as if He had been physically near.

Our God is no less powerful today. Though not physically present, He sovereignly controls events in the lives of believers. We must not hesitate to call upon Him. In 1 John we read, "This is the confidence we have in approaching God: that if we ask anything according to his will, he hears us. And if we know that he hears us—whatever we ask—we know that we have what we asked of him" (1 John 5:14–15).

Where do you hurt today? Acknowledge your need to Jesus and seek His mercy in meeting that need. Though sometimes He seems far away, He is closer than you think.

Meditation Time-Out

1. Why do we hesitate to confess our insufficiency?
2. What need has the Lord met in your life this week?
3. How does Jesus meet your needs?

MIRACLE AT THE POOL

Read John 5:1–15

Then Jesus said to him, "Get up! Pick up your mat and walk."

John 5:8

With twenty-eight seconds remaining, Boston College trailed the Miami Hurricanes 45–41, and the situation looked hopeless—except to Boston College quarterback Doug Flute. The 5′9″ "Miracle Worker" threw four passes, the last one a forty-eight-yard touchdown bomb to Gerard Phelan for an Eagle victory. Even Coach Jack Bicknell was stunned. "I didn't believe it until I saw the kids going nuts," he said. "It was a miracle."

A greater miracle worker once performed an even greater miracle one day in Jerusalem. That was the day when Jesus was attracted to a man who had been crippled for thirty-eight years. Not only was Jesus attracted to him, but He also healed the man, revealing Himself as *Jehovah Rapha*—the God that heals (Exodus 15:26). Notice three important aspects of this healing.

First, Jesus asked the man if he really *wanted* to be healed. This question sounds strange at first, but in light of the fact that a high percentage of hospital beds could be vacated if people really desired to be well, it is a valid one. Many people actually become attached to their condition. Psychosomatic illness becomes a way of life.

Second, Jesus purposely performed this miracle on the Jewish Sabbath, proving that the day was made for man's good and not the other way around. This act provoked public opposition to Jesus; previously He had enjoyed the support of the religious leaders. Now that He voided their list of dos and don'ts, they became His enemies (v. 16).

109

Finally, though Jesus did not say that this particular suffering was a result of the man's sin, many disabilities are direct consequences of disobedience to God's Word. Venereal disease, the trauma resulting from abortion, and the inner turmoil caused by jealousy and hatred are examples. The Lord warned that only by being set free from sin could the man avoid a worse end (v. 14). Inward cleansing from sin is a greater miracle than outward healing and much better than a winning touchdown with no time remaining!

Meditation Time-Out

1. Do you really want to be free of sin?
2. What sin are you aware of that has caused suffering?
3. Which is more important, doing good or honoring a day?

EQUAL WITH GOD!

Read John 5:16–30

. . . he was even calling God his own Father, making himself equal with God.

John 5:18

While some athletes boast of their skill and success on the playing field, most outstanding performers are hesitant to "toot their own horn." They know that competition is great. There are no competitors or teams who are so perfect that they can't be defeated on any given day. That's what attracts spectators to sporting events.

There was one man who had every right to lay claim to greatness, however. Jesus Christ not only deserved to be worshiped as God, but He also left no doubt in the minds of His listeners about His claims. His words were crystal clear, and His actions backed them to the hilt. He claimed to be equal with God *in nature* because He was the Son of God (v. 18). All of God is revealed in Jesus. His person and work declares the very nature of the Father.

He claimed to be equal with God in power, and He depended totally on the Father (v. 19). God alone has power over life and death and because Jesus was God, He could give life to whoever He chose.

He claimed to be equal with God in authority (v. 22), and because of His submission to the Father, He has all authority to judge both the living and the dead. One day He will judge the whole world (Acts 17:31).

Either His claims were true or they were false. If false, Jesus was either deceived or intentionally lying. But His actions consistently backed His every word. Even the Roman governor, Pilate, declared he could find no basis for charges against Jesus (John 18:38).

Therefore, His claims must be true. We can accept Him by faith as Savior and Lord, or we can reject Him by active rebellion or passive indifference. But let us not think that He left any doubt about who He claimed to be. He's the only man who ever lived with a legitimate claim to personal glory!

Meditation Time-Out

1. What do you know about God?
2. How do you know it?
3. What did Jesus' work have to do with His person?

RELIABLE WITNESSES

Read John 5:31–47

"If I testify about myself, my testimony is not valid."

John 5:31

A crew of reliable officials can make or break a ball game, for they must carefully observe what happens before making a wise decision on the play. In basketball and football, officials who let play get out of hand can lose control of the game and ruin the fun for everyone. In baseball, an umpire who anticipates a call of "safe" or "out" before it occurs will make wrong calls and rule unfairly. A man must first be a reliable witness of the action and then decide accordingly.

In John 5:31, Jesus was not saying that He had "made a bad call" or that His witness about Himself was unreliable (John 8:14), but rather that it would not be accepted by men. Therefore, other witnesses to His lordship are given to men to encourage trust in Him. Five of these are listed in verses 31–47.

The first witness listed is that of John the Baptist. This tough-minded individual went ahead of Jesus and proclaimed not himself, but the coming Lord.

Greater than John were the works Jesus performed that confirmed Him as God's Son. Seven are recorded in John's gospel. He healed the sick, raised the dead, and turned water into wine. These miracles were written down that "by believing you may have life in his name" (John 20:31).

The Father Himself is the third witness of Christ's deity, "For God was pleased to have all his fullness dwell in him (Colossians 1:19). God put His stamp of approval on His Son.

The fourth reliable witness which testifies of Jesus is the written Word. Though it is completely accurate and holy, we should not worship the written Word. Scripture points us to the person who is worthy of worship. If we know God, we will love to study His Word to discover more about Him.

The fifth reliable witness is the first five books of the Old Testament, the books written by Moses. Though the Jews claimed to believe Moses, they rejected Jesus. Such rejection is a contradiction, for Moses wrote of Christ!

A reliable testimony of who Jesus is and what He can do is very powerful. Down through history, millions of people have met the Lord Jesus and have witnessed His love and forgiveness. If you are one of these, don't discount the impact of your testimony. Share it whenever God gives you the opportunity.

Meditation Time-Out

1. What has Jesus done for you?
2. How does His work confirm His claims?
3. How often do you share Him with others?

TRAINING TABLE
FOR FIVE THOUSAND

Read John 6:1–15

Jesus then took the loaves, gave thanks, and distributed to those who were seated as much as they wanted. He did the same with the fish.

John 6:11

K nowing the importance of regular, well-balanced meals, many major college athletic programs provide a training table for their athletes. The food is appealing and nutritious, and players are encouraged to eat all they want. Because some players are lax in coming to each meal, a checklist is kept, and athletes are required to sign in at every meal. This is for their welfare and for the good of the team.

In John 6, Jesus miraculously provided a training meal for five thousand men. This miracle is the only one recorded in all four Gospels. To give this physical sign that He was the Bread of Life, He produced enough food for all of them from five small barley loaves and two fish. Let's examine how Jesus orchestrated this miracle. First of all, He made the disciples responsible and accountable. He didn't ask for volunteers. Once made accountable, they realized their lack of resources. Then, we learn from Mark 6:39–40 that the Lord organized the crowd into groups of fifty to one hundred to make distribution easier. Evidently, Jesus was an organized person.

In total dependence upon the Father, He gave thanks to God and broke the loaves. No miracle occurred until they were broken. In the same way, no miraculous signs of His power are manifested until we come to the place of having our independence from God broken and realizing our dependence upon Him. We can feel safe in giving up all to serve and obey Him, for the boy who gave the loaves and fish never missed a bite of lunch.

Finally, Jesus was never wasteful. He instructed the disciples to collect the leftovers (v. 12). Now at the highest point of His popularity, Jesus proved Himself to be *Jehovah Rohi,* the Shepherd of His people who is the all-sufficient One. He still meets our every need today.

Meditation Time-Out

1. How is Jesus all-sufficient for you?
2. What have you given to Him that He has multiplied?
3. For what has God appointed you and made you responsible?

TRAINING CAMP AT SEA

Read John 6:16–24

. . . they saw Jesus approaching the boat, walking on the water; and they were terrified.

John 6:19

S wimmer Don Schollander went through a tough period of training in preparation for the Olympics. Showing promise in the pool, he left his Oregon home after his freshman year of high school to train in California with the Santa Clara Swim Club. At 6:30 A.M., he would warm up with a 500-meter (one-third mile) swim. Then he swam another 500 meters, using only his arms! Next were 100-meter repeats, another distance swim, more repeats, breathing drills, turning drills, starting drills, and one more long swim. The afternoon workout lasted even longer—two hours—and was more of the same. In his book *Deep Water,* Don related that at the peak of training, he was swimming about eight miles a day!

Jesus chose a strenuous workout to train His disciples, too. In fact, Mark 6:45 records that He actually sent them into a storm. In His sovereignty He knew beforehand what they were going to go through and how He would meet their need. Sure enough, sometime between 3 and 6 A.M. things looked pretty bleak. More than three miles away from shore, one of those sudden, severe storms, common on the Sea of Galilee, erupted. Jesus knew their fear and walked out to calm them. Matthew 14 records that Peter walked a short way outside the boat when he recognized the Lord, but his faith gave way, and he started to sink. Jesus rescued Peter, got into the boat, and evidently performed another miracle, for the boat immediately arrived at their destination on the opposite shore.

Our Lord went to great lengths to reveal Himself to His disciples. Here He is *El Elyon*—possessor of heaven and earth. He is the same God to us. He knows our future trials. In fact, He allows them in our lives. Yet, He is always near to rescue us. Furthermore, our complete deliverance from trials—reaching the opposite shore of this life—will come soon, much more quickly than we realize. Are you trusting Him until that day?

Meditation Time-Out

1. What storm has God allowed you to experience?
2. How has He brought you through?
3. What have you learned from it?

BREAD THAT SATISFIES

Read John 6:25–59

"I am the bread of life. He who comes to me will never go hungry, and he who believes in me will never be thirsty."

John 6:35

Sometimes athletes attempt to satisfy a large appetite with between-meal snacks. Soft drinks, french fries, and doughnuts tempt their natural desire. Then, when it is time for a good training meal, junk food has diminished the appetite for what really satisfies. Continuously eating this way reduces physical efficiency and detracts from performance.

The same is true in the spiritual realm. Feeding on a diet provided by the world and not upon the things of the Spirit of God will cause a similar drop in the quality of life. Only by feeding upon the true Bread of Life, Jesus Christ, can we find contentment. Notice how the True Bread contrasts with man's junk food. The people wanted Jesus because He filled their physical stomachs; they thought they should do something to keep Him around (v. 28). He made it clear that the only work desired by God is to believe on the One God had sent (v. 29). Instead of seeing to believe, God asked that they believe and then see. In fact, the one they needed was not a commodity but a person—Jesus Himself. All they needed was to believe Him to enjoy the very bread of life!

Finally, Jesus promised that whoever came to Him would find complete satisfaction. He promised that He would never drive away those who came to Him (v. 37), that they would never be lost (v. 39), and that He would raise them up at the last day (v. 44). All who come to Him remain in Him, just as He remains in them (v. 56). What a great promise of permanent fulfillment!

Do you hunger for the true Bread of Life? Don't try to satisfy that God-given drive with the junk food of this world. Feed upon the Lord Jesus, and you will be satisfied.

Meditation Time-Out

1. What "junk food" do men substitute for Christ?
2. What do you do to feed upon Jesus?
3. How long does the satisfaction of feeding upon Him last?

DISSENSION ON THE TEAM

Read John 6:60–71

"You do not want to leave too, do you?" Jesus asked the Twelve.

John 6:67

M orale problems not only ruin the fun of participation for everyone concerned, but greatly diminish the performance of a team. Solutions vary with the circumstances, but often a player either leaves the team on his own, or he must be dismissed. A good coach can read the spirit of most players even though no words are spoken. He must deal with the attitude immediately, because problems are not solved by ignoring them.

Like any good coach, Jesus could read dissension in the hearts of some of His followers. When He started teaching the hard truths about salvation and His sacrifice, many forsook Him. His popularity as a political figure who would deliver Israel from Rome was over. As on any athletic team, doubt and dissension became infectious, and many stumbled. He even read the doubts in the minds of some of the disciples. Though Judas, who never trusted Christ in the first place, was one of the twelve disciples, Jesus knew he would betray Him (v. 70). The Master did everything possible to show him the way of salvation. Yet, he would not respond and eventually "cut himself from the team." Even the Perfect Coach did not reach everyone!

Our Lord also offered the other eleven disciples the opportunity to defect. He could read in their eyes their misgivings about His claims, and He did not desire forced loyalty. Quick to reply, Peter responds, "Lord, to whom shall we go? You have the words of eternal life. We believe and know that you are the Holy One of God" (vv. 68–69).

121

The disciples knew they were on the winning team. If you are thinking of leaving Him, you would be wise to think about the alternatives. There is no other source of life; He is the only Savior.

Do you have a spirit of trust in the Lord, even though you may not understand all His teachings? Hang in there by faith. There is no other "team" worthy of your loyalty.

Meditation Time-Out

1. Have you had misgivings about the Lord?
2. How did you handle them?
3. What do you understand today that was formerly unclear?

DIVISION IN THE HOUSE

Read John 7:1–24
For even his own brothers did not believe in him.

John 7:5

O ften Christian athletes look at their ball clubs and discover they are in the minority, even totally alone, in their walk with the Lord. No one else turns down the booze, refuses to live by the world's ideas of right and wrong, and has a heart for worshiping God. Though deep down he is much respected and often even envied by the crowd, the Christian is ostracized.

Jesus was in the same minority situation as a Christian athlete. At the Jewish Feast of Tabernacles—a feast celebrating God's presence with the Jews during the Exodus—the custom was to live in booths of tree branches for seven days. Jesus' half brothers pressured the Lord to prove himself to the nation and to themselves at this feast. Though they had lived with Him for over thirty years, they still did not believe in Him. Yet, they had no reason not to believe His claims. He had lived a sinless life for all that time. He had demonstrated love and obedience to His earthly parents. Even so, He was still alone in His own family. Thirty years of perfect example did not cause one brother to believe in Him. Halfway through the feast, His teaching caused further amazement among His brothers and other Jews (vv. 14–15). Though they were trying to kill Him, it was not yet time for His date with the cross (v. 19).

Are you the only one on your team or in your family who has trusted Christ? The truth is often divisive, isn't it? Remember, God has put you where you are for the very purpose of being a light so that others might believe. Don't be discouraged if you are the only one. Jesus knows the feeling and will constantly give you strength to stand.

Meditation Time-Out

1. In what situation are you the only Christian?
2. How did Jesus relate to those who did not believe?
3. By what authority did Jesus teach?

THE RIGHT
TIME AND PLACE

Read John 7:25–44

"If anyone is thirsty, let him come to me and drink. Whoever believes in me, as the Scripture has said, streams of living water will flow from within him."

John 7:37–38

T ight end Marv Fleming had a reputation for being in the right place at the right time. Fleming made the Green Bay Packer squad in 1963 and played in two Super Bowls (in 1967 and 1968). Traded to Miami in 1970, he was on three more Super Bowl teams in 1972, 1973, and 1974! That's five Super Bowl appearances, more than any other pro player.

The Lord Jesus was always in the right place, at the right time, with just the right word. The last day of the Feast of Tabernacles was the right time for the proclamation of Himself as Messiah. For seven days the Jews had walked to the pool of Siloam, filled pitchers with water, and taken the pitchers to the temple. On the way they sang Psalms 103 through 118, reminding themselves of God's miraculous provision for their nation during the Exodus wanderings. As they entered the temple, the water was poured out upon the altar. In this way, God's past faithfulness and His coming kingdom were kept in the forefront of their minds. On the last day of the feast, Jesus stood (the rabbis usually taught from a sitting position) and boldly announced that those who thirsted could come to Him for water that would permanently satisfy.

Anyone could come to Him; the only requirement was that the person have a thirst for true spiritual fulfillment.

God has so designed us that we all have a spiritual thirst for Him. When we come to Him, He promises not only to fill us but to cause an overflow of blessing from our innermost being to others. There must be both intake and outflow of God's Spirit so that we never become stagnant. God's way of providing permanent satisfaction to man was announced by Jesus at the best time and at the most appropriate place.

Meditation Time-Out

1. Why did the Jews easily understand Jesus' claims?
2. What requirements did Jesus give to receive "living water"?
3. When has "living water" flowed from your life to others?

IRONY AND A UNIQUE MAN

Read John 7:45–53

"No one ever spoke the way this man does."

John 7:46

T he Notre Dame–Southern Cal college football series has been exciting. In 1974, USC trailed 24–6 at halftime but scored 49 points in the first seventeen minutes of the second half for a 55–24 victory. Notre Dame had allowed only eight touchdowns in ten previous games, and USC got eight in less than twenty minutes! Ten years earlier, in 1964, the Trojans had rallied from a 17–0 halftime deficit for a 20–17 win. Ironically, both games were played in the Los Angeles Coliseum and the opposing coaches—John McKay and Ara Parseghian—were the same. The 1964 game was Ara's first loss, the 1974 game his final loss as Irish head coach!

There was also great irony in the response of religious leaders to Jesus. When the temple guards returned to the chief priests and Pharisees without arresting Him, they admitted that "No one ever spoke the way this man does." Many people retained a favorable opinion of Him and yet refused to accept Him as Messiah.

The Pharisees' prideful retort that no religious leaders believed in Him was ironic because a number of them soon did believe in Him (John 12:42). They were jealous of His great popularity (John 12:19).

The Pharisees accused the common man of ignorance of the Law and of being under a curse. Skillfully, Nicodemus pointed out that they were disobeying the law in condemning Jesus without a hearing. The Pharisees were under a curse for not believing God's own Son (John 3:36).

Finally, in dodging Nicodemus' question, they asserted that a prophet does not come from Galilee. Ironically, both Jonah and Nahum had come from Galilee. Evidently, the Pharisees were not as wise as they would have had people believe!

There is this irony in every person who rejects the claims of God's unique Son. The only logical response to Jesus Christ is to fall at His feet in worship and faith. Only then does a man become consistent and rational in his thinking!

Meditation Time-Out

1. How is Jesus unique?
2. What is ironic about rejecting His claims?
3. Why is worship the only logical response to Jesus?

FORGIVENESS:
THE RIGHT WAY OUT

Read John 8:1–11

"Then neither do I condemn you," Jesus declared. "Go now and leave your life of sin."

John 8:11

Detroit manager Sparky Anderson could have been vindictive after winning the World Series in 1984. Six years earlier, he had been fired by Cincinnati, where he had led the Reds to five pennants. But with a touch of class, he said, "We had finished second in both 1977 and '78. The best way they [the managers] could shock them [the fans] was to get the No. 1 guy, me. Maybe their decision was right. I had some faults."

Sparky is not the only one who knows how to forgive. Jesus, the author of forgiveness, shows how it's done in John 8. Malicious and deceitful Pharisees had trapped a woman in adultery and attempted to use her to trap Jesus. Had they really been interested in applying the law, they would have brought the guilty man to Jesus also (Leviticus 20, Deuteronomy 22). Thinking they had the Lord in a bind, they asked what should be done to the woman. If He said to free her, He would go against Moses' law. If He recommended stoning her to death, he would be labeled a heartless teacher and discredited.

However, Jesus was not trapped. He patiently bent over and wrote something in the sand. He may have been listing the very sins of the accusers, or He may have been giving them time to see their inconsistency and leave, but in either case He exposed their hypocrisy. He said for the sinless among them to throw the first stone. Because all are sinners, no one could stone her! Halley writes: "It is, no doubt, just as hard, perhaps harder, for God to forgive our respectable, refined, polite, selfish, snobbish sins, as it is for Him to forgive the grosser sins of the poor souls that have lost in the battle of life."

Thank God, we have a kind and tender Savior. He who forgave the adulterous woman will forgive us, too. Therefore, we must not only forgive others, but we must also forgive ourselves of all confessed sin. Only through forgiveness are bitterness and regret removed.

Meditation Time-Out

1. How does forgiving someone help you?
2. What does forgiving yourself do for your relationships?
3. What basis do you have to forgive yourself and others?

LIGHT AND DARKNESS

Read John 8:12–30

"I am the light of the world. Whoever follows me will never walk in darkness, but will have the light of life."

John 8:12

T here is one thing that will always stop a nighttime football game—light failure. The game goes on in rain, snow, sleet, or cold weather, but when the lights fail, the party's over. No plays can be run without the lights. In fact, it's even difficult to tell teammate from opponent in the dark.

Lights were also important at the Jewish Feast of Tabernacles. A major feature was the lighting of giant lamps in the temple courtyard. The wicks of the lamps were made of worn-out robes of the priests. They were lighted to remind Israel of the guidance of God during the wilderness wanderings—He had led them by a moving cloud during the day which became a pillar of fire at night.

Appropriately, Jesus again spoke to the people concerning His identity. He claimed to be the light of the whole world, a true picture of God and holiness. This light is surely needed by a world hopelessly floundering in sin, ignorance, and evil. Jesus promised that those who follow Him will never walk in darkness but will have the very light of life.

Notice that this light is not of the world but comes from outside it. Nothing in this world produces light. Only God can provide the eternal light and life for man. Also, those who do not accept Christ are in darkness. No matter how great their knowledge or position, any person who rejects the Son of God is hopelessly lost. Finally, people who reject God's light will die in their sins. Jesus states three times in this chapter, in verse 21 and twice in verse 24, that people who reject the Light die in their sins. They cannot go where He dwells.

Just as a well-lighted field is essential for a night game, so the Light of the world is needed for salvation from sin in this dark world. Jesus is that Light. Are you following Him?

Meditation Time-Out

1. How has Jesus been light to you?
2. Why do those in darkness challenge the Light?
3. Why can God not allow darkness in Heaven?

WHO IS YOUR DAD?

Read John 8:31–47

"You belong to your father, the devil, and you want to carry out your father's desire."

John 8:44

It is often easy to spot the son of a professional baseball player or a coach by the way he walks onto a ballfield. Such a player is usually well schooled in the fundamentals of the game, and some of the father's talent has been passed on. Many times, the son of an ex-pro is good enough to make the big time. Examples include Terry Francona, Dale Berra, Cal and Billy Ripken, Ossie Virgil, and Buddy Bell.

When the Jews claimed God as their Father in Jesus' day, He boldly asserted the truth: their walk did not uphold their claim. Because of their persecution of God's Son, they could not be children of God or even spiritual children of Abraham, for the great patriarch faithfully trusted God. The Jewish religious leaders failed to trust God or His Word and, in their unbelief, were blind to reality. When Jesus offered them freedom, they claimed to never having been in bondage to anyone, forgetting about long periods of slavery in Egypt, in Babylon, and currently under the Romans. Like many today, they denied reality and had no sense of their own sin. As natural men, they did not receive the teaching of God's Spirit (1 Corinthians 2:14).

Jesus plainly told them that their rejection of Him proved that their real father was Satan. As an athletic son reflects his father's physical traits, they reflected Satan's spiritual traits of lying (Satan originated lying in the Garden of Eden), murder (Satan invited Cain to murder his brother Abel), and pride (Satan fell from heaven because of pride).

Thank God that we have a Savior who plainly tells us where we stand. Either a man is a son of God by faith in Christ, or he is a son of the devil. There is no alternative.

Meditation Time-Out

1. Why is natural man a son of the devil?
2. In what ways does man deny reality?
3. Why was Jesus so bold in declaring the truth?

A BOLD CLAIM

Read John 8:48–59

"I tell you the truth," Jesus an-swered, "before Abraham was born, I am!"

John 8:58

Every year a weekly poll of college football coaches and writers is taken to rank the nation's best teams. The polls make for interest-ing controversy; several fine teams annually claim to be deserving of the top ranking. Even after the bowl season ends on January 1, there are often two or three bold claims for the top spot. A final poll settles the issue but not always the debate.

Jesus Christ continually made the bold assertion that He was God. He said He existed before Abraham, who lived centuries earlier (v. 58). He identified Himself as the eternal, unchanging God, the "I AM" of Exodus 3:14. He left no doubt of who He claimed to be.

The Jews had two choices: they could call Him a blasphemer and kill Him, or they could fall at His feet and worship Him as the Lord God Almighty. Logic dictated He could not possibly be just another teacher of religion. He was God or He was a liar.

Many through history have acknowledged His deity. Some believe that Napoleon said, "I know men, and I tell you, Jesus is not a man. He commands us to believe, and gives no other reason than His awful word, I AM GOD." Many rejected Jesus completely. He was maligned and scorned and would have been killed on the spot had He not slipped away.

Though Jesus honored God in everything, He was dishonored by man. God promises to honor those who honor Him (1 Samuel 2:30), but He does not promise that those who honor Him will be honored by man.

135

The Lord Jesus chose to honor and glorify the Father, and as a result, men turned away from Him. After escaping from their wrathful intentions on this occasion, Jesus never again pleaded with Israel. They had completely rejected their Messiah. They had driven away their God, and they didn't even recognize Him.

Meditation Time-Out

1. How clear to the Jews were the claims of Christ?
2. Why could Jesus not be *only* a great moral teacher?
3. What might it cost you to honor God?

HANDICAPPED
FOR GOD'S GLORY

Read John 9:1–12

". . . but this happened so that the work of God might be displayed in his life."

John 9:3

I n victory or defeat, a good coach will analyze each game to discover cause and effect. By analyzing the causes, he can make adjustments to reinforce desirable results or to correct past mistakes. The final goal is to improve future performance, which should result in more victories.

Jesus' disciples asked, "Why?" when they encountered a blind man in John 9. Not only did the Lord give a direct answer—to display the work of God—but He also healed the man. In fact, Jesus was fulfilling the prophecy of Isaiah 42:7 which said the Messiah would restore sight to the blind. He healed eyesight on four recorded occasions—Matthew 9, Mark 8, Luke 18, and John 9—each time using a different method. The method was secondary and was patterned to the need of the individual. In this case, the man needed to demonstrate faith and obedience— faith that Jesus could heal him and obedience to wash in the pool of Siloam. In trusting Jesus, he was healed and God's glory was displayed. The very purpose for his blindness was fulfilled that day.

Sometimes unexplainable things happen in our lives. There may be sickness, financial problems, or unavoidable conflict. We ask God, "Why?" Sometimes He doesn't tell us immediately. In fact, unless the suffering is because of our sin, it may be years before we understand His reasons. We may not even understand until we get to heaven. But knowing God, we can be confident in saying yes to His plan for us, realizing that His glory will be the ultimate outcome in every trial.

Meditation Time-Out

1. What was the blind man's attitude toward Jesus?
2. What trial has happened to you which you do not understand?
3. Why do you think God has allowed your trial?

TALK OF THE TOWN

Read John 9:13–34

"Whether he is a sinner or not, I don't know. One thing I do know. I was blind but now I see!"

John 9:25

One would think that most people would be satisfied when their favorite team was successful on the athletic field while demonstrating outstanding character qualities. But listen to ex-UCLA coach John Wooden, basketball's most successful coach of all time. "Those should have been the happiest years for Nell and me. But they weren't. Even after winning all those championships, we really weren't happy. When we won, they said we didn't win by a great enough margin, or that we looked bad winning."

You would think that the people of Jesus' day would have been happy with His gracious teaching and His merciful acts. But no sooner had He healed the man born blind, than the Pharisees investigated the healing in an attempt to discredit the Savior. They accused Him of breaking their Sabbath rules and questioned the authenticity of the miracle He had performed. They tried to talk the man out of his testimony. Like people today, they were willing to hear about God, but when the name of Jesus Christ was mentioned, they took offense. Their proud religious system would not tolerate such miracles, but the man's logical defense of the healing completely upstaged these learned clergymen. When he stuck faithfully to the truth of what had happened, they threw him out of the synagogue. They hated Jesus, His miracles, and all objects of His wonderful work.

John Wooden and the man healed by Jesus discovered the same truth. Some people are never content with success unless they are center stage. The problem in the human heart is not an inability to believe the truth but an unwillingness to accept it.

Meditation Time-Out

1. What was the testimony of the man Jesus healed?
2. Why did the religious rulers hate Him?
3. Who did the Jews really despise?

THE REAL BLIND MEN

Read John 9:35–41

Jesus said, "If you were blind, you would not be guilty of sin; but now that you claim you can see, your guilt remains."

John 9:41

Sometimes the loudest critics of athletes and coaches are those who watch from the stands and possess the least knowledge. It's easy to criticize from off the field. Everything looks easy from the stands! There is no risk involved, and the environment is comfortable. Furthermore, those who have never coached or played are easily tempted to give the competitors and officials a piece of their minds.

In John 9:37, Jesus made one of His most direct statements concerning His deity. Having located the man He had healed, Jesus personally revealed His lordship. Notice the progress of the man's knowledge of Jesus in chapter 9. In verse 17, he realizes Jesus is a prophet. But now, in verse 38, he recognizes Jesus as Lord. The man's response to the revelation of Christ is proper—he worshiped Him.

The Pharisees were another case. Because they thought they had superior knowledge, they became proud and self-centered. Therefore, they were blind to the person and work of Jesus Christ. Sin deceives people so that they live in falsehood and darkness. Because they would only criticize, Jesus pronounced them guilty of sin and therefore in danger of God's judgment.

Meditation Time-Out

1. Why did Jesus seek out the man He had healed?

2. Why did Jesus say the Pharisees were blind?
3. What is required for a person to have his guilt removed?

OUR MASTER COACH

Read John 10:1–21

"I am the good shepherd. The good shepherd lays down his life for the sheep."

John 10:11

There are many great men in the coaching profession who coach because of a heartfelt concern for others. The lives of young people who compete in athletics are their highest priority. Such coaches sacrifice personally for the glory of God through athletics. In contrast to coaches whose motive is more money and a bigger job, these men serve God by their personal interest in and their kind treatment of players.

Jesus used the parable of a shepherd and his sheep to illustrate His personal concern for the Jewish people and all others who would come to Him. In contrast to the Pharisees (represented by "a stranger" in v. 5, by "thieves and robbers" in v. 8, by "the hired hand" in v. 12), the Good Shepherd came to give abundant life (v. 10). He died for, owns, feeds, protects, keeps, and rewards His sheep. This is in contrast to the false teachers who did not care for the sheep and were only interested in money and self-preservation.

Jesus, therefore, claimed to be the gate to life for all who would come to Him (v. 7). Jesus, the Shepherd, died for the sheep. Notice, He sovereignly and voluntarily lays down His life (vv. 17–18). No one could take it from Him, and no one could prevent His rising from the dead in glory.

The Jews were divided in their opinion of Him. So are people today. Some choose to play for the evil coach, Satan, who cares nothing for his players. He will destroy his own team. In contrast, the Master Coach,

Jesus Christ, died for His players and leads them to abundant life. For which do you play?

Meditation Time-Out

1. What are some traits of the Master Coach?
2. How does the evil coach, Satan, destroy his players?
3. How can people be convinced to play for the Master Coach?

VOICE OF
THE MASTER COACH

Read John 10:22–42

"My sheep listen to my voice; I know them, and they follow Me. I give them eternal life, and they shall never perish; no one can snatch them out of my hand."

John 10:27–28

One of the most frustrating problems for a ball player is to be in a batting slump and have two or three "instructors" give him all kinds of advice. Everyone has an opinion, and confusion results. Instead, a player should listen to only one authority who knows him well and in whom he has confidence.

Two months after His discourse on the good shepherd, Jesus attended the eight-day Feast of Dedication in Jerusalem. When accosted by hostile Jewish leaders, He again used the shepherd/sheep illustration concerning His leadership. He made it clear that there was one true Shepherd, and He claimed to be the one, the very Son of God. Listening to advice from "false shepherds" would only result in confusion.

Eastern shepherds named their sheep, and the sheep came when called. Several flocks were usually mixed overnight inside a city's walls. At daybreak when the shepherd's voice called them, they heard, knew the master's voice, and followed their shepherd out to pasture. Observe some comparisons Jesus makes between sheep and His followers:

1. Jesus' sheep listen to Him (v. 27). God's children are constantly tuned in to His Word for instruction, guidance, and

145

comfort. His sheep follow Him (v. 27). Not only do His sheep hear, but they also obey Him and follow His leadership in various areas of their lives. Following Jesus is their constant delight.

2. Jesus' sheep have eternal life (v. 28). He gives eternal life now, and it lasts forever. Spiritually, the Lord's sheep will never die.

3. Jesus' sheep are secure in His hands (v. 28). They are also secure in the Father's hands (v. 29) and can never be snatched away from Him. What comfort to know that the security of God's children depends upon His mighty power and not upon their feeble efforts.

From this encounter, the Jews had no doubt that Jesus claimed to be God (v. 33). They would have stoned Him had He not escaped to keep His later date on Calvary's cross.

The Master Coach is resurrected from the dead and sitting at His Father's right hand. His voice remains the only authoritative voice we can trust. Will you hear, follow, and rest in Him today?

Meditation Time-Out

1. What did the Jews understand about Christ's claims?
2. Why can a believer in Jesus never perish?
3. How do God's sheep behave?

SWITCHING POSITIONS
FOR A HIGHER PURPOSE

John 11:1–16

"This sickness will not end in death. No, it is for God's glory so that God's Son may be glorified through it."

John 11:4

O ften a coach will ask a player to switch from a position where he has felt comfortable for a long time to another position where he must make adjustments. The reason for the switch is not to make things hard for the player but to improve the performance of the team. Such changes were made by superstars Henry Aaron, Pete Rose, and Mike Schmidt. In spite of the difficulty, these players placed the team's purposes above their own and worked hard to adjust.

Lazarus was a man who was temporarily asked by the Lord to "switch positions" on God's team. The Lord had a much higher purpose for the sickness and death of Lazarus than Lazarus or the disciples realized. Certainly, if God is wiser than man, His judgment of what is needed in our lives must be different from ours. Jesus had previously raised Jarius's daughter (Mark 5) and the widow's son (Luke 7) from the dead, and He was preparing to do the same for His friend Lazarus.

Notice Jesus' response when He was told that His friend was sick. In His sovereign knowledge, Jesus said that the purpose for this illness was the glory of God. Rather than run to his bedside immediately, He delayed for two days. Though He loved the whole family, He made them wait because His purpose was higher than the healing of a man.

How was God glorified through Lazarus' sickness, death, and resurrection? By the deepened faith of those who already trusted Christ (v. 15) and by the conversion of many others as well (v. 45). When God is glorified, we should be satisfied. Though His schedule is often different from ours and we must sometimes wait for answers to prayer, His ways are always best. God sees the end from the beginning and allows nothing to happen to us that we cannot handle (1 Corinthians 10:13). We can thank God, knowing that His plan is right on schedule in our lives.

Meditation Time-Out

1. Why did Jesus delay for two days before responding?
2. When friends suffer, how should we react?
3. Did the disciples understand Jesus' purposes?

EMOTIONS
OF THE MASTER

Read John 11:17–37

When Jesus saw her weeping, and the Jews who had come along with her also weeping, he was deeply moved in spirit and troubled.

John 11:33

The emotion of sorrow is as common in competitive athletics as the emotion of joy. For example, Olympic runner Zola Budd not only lost the women's 3,000 meter run in the 1984 Los Angeles Olympic Games, but was blamed by her idol, Mary Decker, for running into her from behind and knocking her down. Both runners were unable to finish. Though no one officially found fault with Zola's running, she was upset that someone she highly respected would fall and then blame her. She even considered giving up a promising future in international competition.

While walking the earth, Jesus Christ let His emotions be seen on many occasions. When Lazarus died, He was "deeply moved in spirit and troubled." The word used indicates that He had compassion for the family of His friend. Certainly, He is "moved in spirit" in our times of grief. His compassion causes Him to show concern for a sorrowing humanity.

Jesus wept over the tragic consequences of sin. He saw firsthand the effects of man's rebellion against God and the restriction of living in a body tainted by sin. The death that results from sin temporarily marred God's perfect creation.

He was troubled over the hypocritical wailing of the Jews who visited Lazarus' family. According to custom, Jewish mourners came to the home of a deceased person and wailed loudly. This wailing was not from hearts of faith in God and true compassion for the bereaved but was a religious ritual. Such ritual without sincerity greatly troubled Jesus.

Our independent culture needs to learn that men who cry are not unmanly. Often, crying is the only right response to a situation. Jesus wept over Jerusalem's rejection of Him (Luke 19:41) and in prayer before God (Hebrews 5:7). His compassion for man is in stark contrast to the apathy and stoicism of the Greek gods. What a loving and sympathetic God we serve! One day, however, when He returns, He will wipe away every tear (Revelation 21:4). What a glorious day that will be!

Meditation Time-Out

1. What claim did Jesus make about resurrection and life?
2. What promise did Jesus make to those who believe in Him?
3. What did Martha believe about Jesus?

GLORY AND THE STONE

Read John 11:38–44

"Did I not tell you that if you believed, you would see the glory of God?"

John 11:40

During the late 1960s and early 1970s, baseball's College World Series was ruled by the Southern California Trojans. Time after time, they rallied from behind to win national championships—during one stretch winning five CWS titles in a row! On one occasion, USC trailed Minnesota 7–0 with one out in the bottom of the ninth inning. Though managing only one hit off Dave Winfield until then, they rallied for a seemingly impossible 8–7 victory.

While on earth, Jesus raised his friend Lazarus from the dead. He did it not only because of His tender compassion for Lazarus's family and in answer to their prayers, but to prove that He was God's Son and to bring glory to His Father.

Because of the very warm climate and quick decomposition, the Jews usually buried a corpse the same day a man died. Jesus did not arrive on the scene for four days, and when He ordered the stone taken from the entrance, Martha protested. Probably she felt that it was too late and was embarrassed by the smell. Nevertheless, in obedience to the Lord, the stone was removed.

Jesus prayed with thanksgiving. Notice how He thanked God *before* His prayer was answered. Jesus called in a loud voice, "Lazarus, come out" (v. 43). Augustine said that if Jesus had not specified "Lazarus," *everyone* would have risen from their graves. Lazarus appeared, and Jesus commanded the people to unwrap the burial clothes and free the man. It is interesting that He asked the men to do what they could—roll away the stone and unwrap the man—as their part in glorifying God.

The Bible says that the day is coming when "all who are in their graves will hear his voice and come out—those who have done good will rise to live, and those who have done evil will rise to be condemned" (John 5:28–29). For the righteous ones who sleep, that will be the greatest comeback of all!

Meditation Time-Out

1. As an athlete, what is your part in glorifying God?
2. What do you learn about prayer from Lazarus's resurrection?
3. Why did Jesus pray publicly?

PLOT TO KILL JESUS

Read John 11:45–57

So from that day on they plotted to take his life.

John 11:53

Sometimes coaches and scouts discriminate against players who do not fit their mold of an outstanding player. The athlete may execute all the necessary skills, getting the job done in his own unique way, but if he doesn't match what others expect, he may have trouble making a team.

Jesus never quite fit the mold of what the religious leaders wanted in a messiah. They could not deny His great miracles but would not accept Him as King. Therefore, the chief priests under Caiaphas and the Pharisees called a meeting of the Sanhedrin, the Jewish council of seventy members who made religious decisions.

The council would not believe the truth Christ presented because they feared the loss of their religion—a complex system of dos and don'ts designed by men to appease God. If their religious system were abolished, there would be no more need for their jobs as priests. Jesus' claim to be the only way to God made the human priesthood obsolete. Since they were held in high esteem by the people, they would lose the status they enjoyed and would suffer a severe blow to their pride. The religious leaders also feared the loss of corrupt financial gain. They had corrupted the priesthood by using their power to cheat the people.

Finally, they feared that the Romans would interpret acceptance of Christ as rebellion and would destroy the nation of Israel. Therefore, they united in the plot to kill Jesus and made this intention public. The jealous high priest was fearful of Jesus' influence and unwittingly prophesied that Christ would die for the nation. God often uses wicked

153

men without their ever being aware of it, for Christ was put to death not only for the Jews but for all men.

Thank God that He was sovereignly in control all the way to Calvary. Though men rejected His Son because He didn't fit their mold, the death of Christ became the means of our salvation.

Meditation Time-Out

1. What was the effect of the raising of Lazarus?
2. Why didn't Jesus fit the religious leaders' mold?
3. Did the words and works of Christ unite or divide men?

ANOINTED WITH THE BEST

Read John 12:1–11

Then Mary took . . . an expensive perfume; she poured it on Jesus' feet and wiped his feet with her hair.

John 12:3

T hough already named the Heisman Trophy winner for 1983, Mike Rozier refused to give less than his best in practice as Nebraska prepared for the Orange Bowl against Miami. After one workout, an assistant coach commented, "It was just a piddley scrimmage, but he ran like it was the national championship. I wonder how many other Heisman Trophy winners would have been out there, running like that? They might have been looking for a way out of it."

Though she may or may not have been an athlete, Mary also refused to give less than her best. Her gift was given to the Lord Jesus at a farewell dinner hosted by Jesus' friends in His honor. The place was Bethany, a town near Jerusalem, and the time was six days before the death of the Lord. Each of His friends revealed their love for Jesus in different ways. Martha served. Lazarus ate with Him. As usual, Mary worshiped at the feet of Jesus (Luke 10:39; John 11:32). She discerned in her spirit that Jesus was about to die. Therefore, she took a $50 jar of perfume—a working man's wages for one year—and anointed Jesus for burial. Mary generously gave the Lord the best that she had. This would be the only anointing He would receive, for the women who later went to His tomb found it empty!

The disciples, led by Judas, expressed disapproval of Mary's act of worship. However, Jesus defended her because of her heart attitude. It is never wrong to give our best to God, and He promises to honor those who honor Him (1 Samuel 2:30). The Master rebuked Judas, who then slipped out to betray Him.

God's ways are not our ways. While it is right to give to the poor, the real motive of our giving should be to honor God. He alone deserves our worship and our resources. Let us give our best to Him!

Meditation Time-Out

1. How would you have reacted to Mary's gift?
2. Why did Jesus defend Mary?
3. Why did the Jews want to kill Lazarus?

WELCOMED TO DEATH

Read John 12:12–19

Many people . . . went out to meet him.

John 12:18

Fans of athletic teams are, for the most part, inconsistent. As Walt Huntley has put it, "They cheer like mad until you fall, and then their praise will stop." When a team's win-loss record does not meet with expectations, or even if they do not win by a large enough margin, disloyalty and criticism replace devotion and praise. The coaches and players who were touted become targets.

Jesus knew about fickle fans. Always a controversial figure wherever He went, the Lord knew the time to give His life was approaching, and He came right to His enemies. No longer cautious, He was greeted with wild enthusiasm by visitors to Jerusalem when He entered the city for the Passover in fulfillment of Zechariah 9:9. Among the rural people (not among residents of the city), He enjoyed great popularity, for they felt that now He would overthrow hated Roman rule. The raising of Lazarus, His claims of kingship, and the people's desire for material and political success led to their cries of "Hosanna" (save now). Their hopes were based, however, upon frenzied enthusiasm and not upon spiritual discernment. They should have realized the donkey Jesus rode was a sign of peace, not the normal animal a conquering king would ride into a city. Their "enthusiasm" was not true faith, and few really trusted Him. When He didn't meet their expectations, their cries of "Hosanna" became "Crucify Him" only a few days later.

What about your devotion and praise to the Lord? Is it based upon what you feel He should do for you? If you don't get what you want, do you criticize and become disloyal to God? Or do you trust that He is all

He claims to be, a Sovereign God working out His plan in your life? True faith is not fickle but sees His providence in every situation.

Meditation Time-Out

1. What was Jesus' purpose in entering Jerusalem?
2. Why were so many people attracted to Jesus?
3. What was the Pharisees' reaction to the publicity of Jesus' entry?

THE HIGHEST GOAL

Read John 12:20–36

*"But I, when I am lifted up
from the earth, will draw all
men to myself."*

John 12:32

T he pressure to win and the sinful nature of man can combine to produce disaster in college athletic programs. Several schools have been found guilty of massive violations of NCAA rules concerning recruiting and payment of athletes. The temptation to try to win at any cost has led coaches and alumni to lose sight of higher goals and to operate with worldly values. Evidently, it's a chronic problem, as some coaches go from school to school and repeat their illegal deeds.

Our Lord Jesus was also tempted to compromise and adopt the world's value system. In John 12:27, He was troubled as He contemplated bearing our sin on the cross. How glad we should be that He refused to bend God's plan! Because He kept a higher goal in sight, the glory of God, believers now have the sure hope of eternal life.

Notice that even in Christ's going to the cross, God was sovereignly in control. In spite of all the scheming of the Jewish leaders, they could not take His life from Him (John 10:18). He laid it down willingly. He even set the time, for though they had said, "not during the Feast" (Matthew 26:5), Jesus said that His hour had come during Passover (John 12:23). He even dictated the manner of His death (v. 33). They had tried numerous times to stone Him, push Him off a cliff, or otherwise take Him by force, but He fulfilled ancient prophecies by being crucified (Psalms 22; 66).

Out of His death on Calvary came life for millions of believers. Like the seed that is planted and dies to produce new life, He produced an abundant harvest of souls through death. The cross is a curse, a terribly offensive thought. It is offensive to man's morality, for it says he has none. It is offensive to man's philosophy, for it says he cannot make himself righteous. But thanks to the Lord Jesus, the empty cross now becomes a symbol of God's glory and our only hope!

Meditation Time-Out

1. How did Jesus know when and where He would die?
2. What does it mean to "hate your earthly life"?
3. Which goal has the highest priority in your life?

UNBELIEF OF A NATION

Read John 12:37–50

Even after Jesus had done all these miraculous signs in their presence, they still would not believe in him.

John 12:37

S ome teams get no respect from sports fans. It seems that every year, to the delight of their die-hard fans, the Chicago Cubs play good baseball for a period of time before falling into the second division. Many baseball fans wait for and even expect them to collapse before season's end. However, in 1984, the Cubs proved to be legitimate contenders, cinching their divisional championship. Maybe this performance was enough to finally shake off the label of losers.

Our Lord Jesus also did not receive respect or acceptance from most people. The Bible says, "He came to that which was his own, but his own did not receive him" (John 1:11). When Jesus gave His final message in the temple (John 12), He quoted the ancient prophet Isaiah, who long ago predicted the coming of the Messiah. Claiming to be light to mankind, He said that to believe Him was to believe God and that those who had seen Him had also seen the Father (vv. 44-46).

In spite of His proofs, the Jewish nation (as predicted by Isaiah) flatly rejected Him as Messiah. God then ratified their choice by allowing their hearts to become hardened to all truth. This is in line with God's consistent dealing with man. Hebrews 3 warns against the hardness of unbelief. The Bible says that God hardened Pharaoh's heart when he refused to believe God's message through Moses (Exodus 11:9–10). Second Thessalonians 2:11 says that God sends a "powerful delusion" to unbelievers so that they believe Satan's lie if they refuse to accept the Lord Jesus. How sad when men refuse the truth, believe a lie, and suffer eternal separation from God in hell as just punishment.

What is your response to Christ's claims? The only rational choice is to accept Him as your Lord and Savior and be spared condemnation. God has spoken clearly in the person of the Lord Jesus. All men will one day stand before Him as personal Savior or as Judge.

Meditation Time-Out

1. How could Isaiah have known about Jesus?
2. Why did the Jewish nation reject the Lord Jesus?
3. Why did some who believed not confess their faith?

HE STOOPED TO CONQUER

Read John 13:1–17

*"I have set you an example
that you should do as I have
done for you."*

John 13:15

A great boxer of the sixties and seventies, Cassius Clay (Mohammed Ali) was sure to let everyone know how he felt about himself. The self-proclaimed king of boxing boldly predicted knockouts over rivals, often asserting himself to be "the greatest." His style of dancing around the ring while he taunted opponents antagonized the public and earned him the nickname "Louisville Lip."

Our Lord Jesus gave us quite a different example of the attitudes we, as His "teammates," are to have. Knowing the Cross was near, He revealed the heart of a true servant. While the disciples were arguing about who was the greatest among them (Luke 22:24), the Lord took water and a towel and washed their feet. This courtesy was usually done by a servant when guests came for a meal. The hot, dusty roads of Israel made sandled feet dirty. What a site for the angels of heaven as they watched the Creator of all stoop to wash the feet of His fallen creation!

At first Peter protested, knowing his unworthiness. Jesus was not only giving a physical example of humility, but He was also teaching spiritual truth. When the Lord explained the importance of being cleansed spiritually, Peter wanted to be washed all over. Jesus explained that a person who has been bathed (experienced the washing of regeneration) is already clean and needs never to be saved again. He does, however, need to experience daily cleansing of sin to enjoy communion with God (1 John 1:9).

After this incident, the disciples never again argued about who was the greatest. However, the church has not been so wise. Throughout history, leaders have desired power over others and elevation in men's eyes. Jesus' example was one of self-sacrifice and not self-seeking. How much better to follow Him than the proud ways of man.

Meditation Time-Out

1. What made Peter change his mind about having his feet washed?
2. After His example, how did Jesus say we could be blessed?
3. How many people serve others as Jesus served?

BETRAYED
BY A COMPANION

Read John 13:18–32

*"I tell you the truth, one of you
is going to betray me."*

John 13:21

I t happens every year. A coach is counting heavily on a player who
has commited himself to the team. But when school starts, he de-
fects, leaving a vacancy on the squad. Some players drift from school to
school; others drop out and never play again. In either case, the team is
hurt, and adjustments must be made because of betrayal by a trusted
player.

Judas was such a player on the Lord's team. He had lived with
Jesus, had heard His words, and had seen His miracles. Probably Judas
had publicly testified to Jesus as Messiah. But he was a thief, and Jesus
knew it when He appointed him executive treasurer of the group. He
wanted this well-thought-of businessman to see himself as he was and
repent. Even at their last meal together, Jesus gave Judas honor by giving Him bread at the head of the table. When Judas departed to betray
Jesus, the disciples still thought well of him. Only Jesus knew He was
being sold out by a friend in fulfillment of prophecy (Psalm 41:9). This
made our Lord very sad (v. 21).

Clearly Judas never really trusted Christ as personal Savior in all the
years they spent together. When the other disciples called Jesus "Lord"
(Matthew 26:22), Judas addressed Him as "rabbi" or "teacher" (v. 25).
Because Judas was never washed, Jesus said he was not clean (John
13:10–11). Our Lord referred to Judas as a devil (John 6:70–71) and a
son of perdition (John 17:12 KJV).

There are unsaved people like Judas in the best of churches. They may identify with the church, even testify of God's goodness, and yet never know Christ as personal Savior. God alone knows their heart attitude. Because men choose darkness, God ratifies their choice, and they suffer the consequences of separation from God. This makes the Heavenly Father very sad. On the other hand, God's children are children of light (1 Thessalonians 3:5). Whosoever will may come to Jesus (Revelation 22:17). Come today and enjoy the light of Jesus Christ.

Meditation Time-Out

1. How could the other disciples not suspect Judas?
2. How did Jesus reveal who would betray Him?
3. Why did Jesus allow Judas to be a disciple?

JESUS' PEP TALK

Read John 13:33–14:4

"And if I go and prepare a place for you, I will come back and take you to be with me that you also may be where I am."

John 14:3

O utstanding coaches have a way of meeting a discouraging situation with great hope. They are able to look through trouble and see "light at the end of the tunnel." In fact, some feel that most great teams are born out of adversity. Through the positive outlook of a great coach, young men are directed to fix their eyes not on a depressing situation (losses, injuries, etc.), but on possibilities for the future. Teams that have done this have experienced great achievements.

Often when things appeared the darkest, our Lord Jesus spoke His greatest words of comfort and hope. In spite of His recent command to love one another (which should have overruled all division and bitterness), He had predicted Peter's flat denial. The disciples were completely bewildered and discouraged. They realized that Jesus was leaving, and no earthly kingdom was immediately forthcoming. Judas had just left to betray Jesus. Everything seemed on the verge of collapse.

Like any great coach, Jesus had just the right words for the situation. In one of His best loved and most remembered pep talks, He instructed His men not to be troubled. He told them to trust God and to keep on trusting Him. Then He gave a promise in which believers of all ages find comfort. He promised to return to take us to be with Him.

When things seem to fall apart, we need to remember heaven, the real home of all believers. One look at the place He is preparing for us will wipe away all tears. Though He spoke the universe into existence, He has spent two thousand years preparing heaven for us.

While He prepares a place for us, He is also busy preparing us for that place. We are in school here on earth, learning to trust Him in each situation and proving His faithfulness in the laboratory of life. Because He is trustworthy, let us trust Him amid life's darkest circumstances.

Meditation Time-Out

1. Why was the situation distressing for the disciples?
2. What was the theme of Jesus' pep talk?
3. How does His talk help you today?

GOD'S WAY OR NO WAY

Read John 14:5–14

*"I am the way and the truth
and the life. No one comes to
the Father except through me."*

John 14:6

I n baseball, there are several ways a team can score runs. A man may score as a result of a hit, an error, or a sacrifice. Others may score on walks, wild pitches, a hit batsman, or even a stolen base. Each way is valid and counts exactly the same. Though most teams have a certain style, all teams score in most of these ways sooner or later.

In the game of life, however, the stakes are much higher and the way to success more exacting. In fact, the Lord Jesus ruled out all other ways to heaven when He claimed to be the only way. Jesus did not claim to be a "way show-er," but the very way itself. His claim excludes all other religious systems and leaders as ways to heaven and happiness. Therefore, it is impossible to trust Jesus plus any other man or system to achieve eternal life (Acts 4:12).

Not only did Jesus claim to be the only way to God, but He also claimed to be the truth able to set men free. Many men can say, "I teach the truth," but Jesus said, "I *am* the truth." Colossians 2:3 says that *all* wisdom and knowledge are hidden in Him. To know Him is to know truth and to be set free (John 8:32). Not to know Him is to live a lie.

Finally, He claimed to be the life that allows us to live forever. Not to trust Him is to be dead in sin and headed for eternal loss. To have Him is to have life (1 John 5:12). His character, His words, and His miracles are all valid evidences of His trustworthiness.

Have you trusted Him? If so, you have the way, the truth, and the life. And you also have a blank check, for He promises to give you whatever you ask for in His name (v. 14). That means you will ask in line with His will and for His glory. The question is, Do you want God to receive glory? Or do you want it for yourself? Because He is the way, the truth, and the life, He deserves and desires all the glory from your life.

Meditation Time-Out

1. Why is Jesus the only way to God?
2. What have you asked for in Jesus' name?
3. How can you glorify God?

THE SPIRIT OF COMFORT

Read John 14:15–31

"And I will ask the Father, and he will give you another Counselor to be with you forever."

John 14:16

When a young person leaves home for the first time, pangs of homesickness often strike. Such was the case with Yankee great Bobby Richardson when he first signed with New York and was sent from his home in Sumter, South Carolina, to the Yankee's farm club in Norfolk, Virginia. Bobby writes in *The Bobby Richardson Story* that he was so homesick he could scarcely perform. Through a letter of comfort from a junior high school coach back home, God encouraged him at a crucial time, and he found strength to persevere.

When Jesus left us in this world to return to His Father, He did not leave us as orphans. He promised another Counselor, One who had the same nature, source, and work of encouragement. In fact, the disciples (and all believers) would now be closer to Him, for verse 17 tells us that He would now dwell *in* them. This coming of the Spirit of truth took place at Pentecost (Acts 2), and He has indwelt every believer since (Romans 8:9). Prior to His coming to dwell permanently in God's people, He had been with them temporarily for special purposes. This new arrangement is far superior and provides the power to express our love to Him by obeying His commands (v. 15). This Holy Spirit comforts us so that even though we are away from our heavenly home, we are not lonely or comfortless.

Our Master Coach didn't leave in bitterness, hatred, or haste. He left in peace, and He willed His peace to us (v. 27). Having made peace with God for us (Romans 5:1), He gave us the peace of God

171

(Philippians 4:7). His peace is not like the world's peace because it does not depend on outward circumstances. The world didn't give us this peace, and the world can never take it away. No matter where we are or what the circumstances of life, our Savior promised that the Spirit would never leave and that His peace would be continuous.

Meditation Time-Out

1. What is the best evidence of your love for Jesus?
2. How long will the Spirit of God stay with us?
3. How does God's peace differ from the world's peace?

PRODUCING
FOR THE MASTER

Read John 15:1–17

"I am the vine; you are the branches. If a man remains in me and I in him, he will bear much fruit; apart from me you can do nothing."

John 15:5

Fifteen-year-old Mary Lou Retton, the West Virginia girl with the Pepsodent smile, captured the hearts of Americans during the 1984 Olympics by winning three gold medals in gymnastic competition. Her formula for success was no secret, however. As everyone knew, she had the most outstanding coach in world class gymnastics. Romanian Bela Karolyi, who had developed 1976 Olympic heroine Nadia Comeneci, had fled communism to live in the USA. He "adopted" Mary Lou, and as she gave him undivided attention, loyalty, and obedience, the expert instructor turned her into an Olympic champion. It is doubtful that she would have performed as well had not Karolyi been her coach.

Our Lord Jesus is also concerned about performance in the lives of His followers. In a discussion on production in John 15, the Master Coach calls Himself the true vine that produces much fruit through its branches. Producing the Christlike qualities of love, joy, peace, and patience (Galatians 5:22–23) in the lives of His followers is the specialty of the Master Coach. This fruit-bearing takes time and requires that we stay in intimate fellowship with Him. Like Mary Lou Retton and her coach, we are totally dependent upon Him to produce fruit in us.

Jesus makes it clear that dead branches like Judas, who *profess* but never *possess* a saving knowledge of Christ, are fruitless and are thrown into the fire to be burned. Certainly, God is very much like a coach who demands a healthy return on His investment. Even fruitful branches who do possess salvation are "pruned" that they may produce more fruit to the glory of God. This process is often painful in the life of the believer, but the result brings great glory to the Father.

Meditation Time-Out

1. How did Jesus say we could bear fruit?
2. Why does Jesus call us His friends?
3. Is the fruit God produces temporary or permanent?

EXPECTED OPPOSITION

Read John 15:18–16:4

"If you belonged to the world, it would love you as its own. As it is, you do not belong to the world, but I have chosen you out of the world. That is why the world hates you."

John 15:19

B ecause of a fallen human nature, the fan in the stands can be a bitter critic of those competing in the game. A great player like George Foster goes into a slump at the plate and draws boos from the home crowd. A fine coach like Rey Dempsey shows concern for the eternal lives of players and is pressured by opposition. Or an infielder like Tom Foli becomes a star, praises God who gave him the ability to play, and the interviewer quickly pulls the microphone away. There is definite opposition when sports heroes either don't succeed on the field or try to lift up the Lord in the eyes of others.

Surprised? We shouldn't be. Jesus warned that the world would *hate* us. James drew a distinct line between the world and the people of God (James 4:4). What is meant by "the world"? It's simply the satanic system of a beautifully arranged and attractively organized society designed to function without God. The world system includes morality and religion. In fact, first-century believers were persecuted, not because they worshiped Jesus, but because they refused to worship other gods along with Him! They were crucified, burned, and thrown to lions because they insisted He was the *only* God worthy of worship. The world will tolerate morality, but when the subject of the deity of Jesus Christ and His sacrifice on the cross for sin is presented, there will be opposition from everywhere. People will discuss their church membership or their parents' background, but discussing a personal relationship with Christ is quite another matter.

Why does the world hate us? Because it hates Him. The Lord Jesus was hated from birth—Herod murdered hundreds of babies in an effort to kill Him—until death. He is hated because His life and words convict of sin. We are hated because of our identification with Jesus. In Muslim countries, when one accepts Christ, his family is responsible for killing him. If they don't do it, the town will. In America, when one accepts Christ, lives for Him, and talks about Him, society turns a cold shoulder. Persecution takes the form of intimidation and subtle ridicule.

Such persecution proves our faith is real. We have been delivered from the darkness of this world and placed into the kingdom of the Son of God (Colossians 1:13). We have new life, new purpose, new hope, and new joy. Because the world knows nothing of these riches, we expect scorn and gladly accept it for His sake.

Meditation Time-Out

1. What is "the world"?
2. How does the kingdom of this world differ from the kingdom of God?
3. Why does the world hate believers?

THE ROLE PLAYER

Read John 16:5–15

"When he comes, he will convict the world of guilt in regard to sin and righteousness and judgment. . . . He will guide you into all truth."

John 16:8, 13

There are certain players in every good club who are used sporadically and at various positions. They are often pressed into service at a moment's notice and asked to fulfill different roles at different times. These athletes are referred to as "role players." In the 1984 World Series, utility man Kurt Bevacqua of San Diego was a role player. As the designated hitter in game two, he hit a timely home run to win an exciting contest.

Though never a "second stringer," the Holy Spirit plays different roles in the lives of unbelievers than He plays in the life of a believer. Because Jesus departed, He sent the Spirit of God to carry on His work in us. There is no jealousy between these two personalities of the godhead; the Spirit always directs us to Christ.

The Spirit's role to the world is first to convict of sin. Many people will admit to vices, failure, mistakes, even crimes. But to confess sin against a Holy God is unthinkable to them. The basic sin—unbelief in Jesus as God's only Son who died for them—can be confessed only as a result of the Spirit's work. Second, the Spirit convicts the world of Jesus' perfect righteousness. The Resurrection was proof that Jesus was God and that His righteousness is available to all (v. 10). Third, the Spirit convicts men that refusal to believe results in condemnation with

Satan, who awaits execution in the lake of fire (Revelation 20:7–10). Only in Christ does man escape that same condemnation.

To the believer, however, the role of the Spirit is very different. He guides us into all truth (v. 13). He reveals God's will in line with the written Word. He does not elevate Himself, but always glorifies the Lord Jesus (v. 14). What a Comforter! Though we may not understand it all, Christians are now better off because Jesus returned to the Father (v. 7).

Meditation Time-Out

1. What is the role of God's Spirit in your life?
2. How are believers better off since Jesus is in heaven?
3. How does the Spirit glorify Christ?

STRATEGY FOR
THE SECOND HALF

Read John 16:16–33

*"I have told you these things,
so that in me you may have
peace. In this world you will
have trouble. But take heart! I
have overcome the world."*

John 16:33

T he halftime intermission is a great chance for the football coach to make adjustments in his game plan. During this important break, it is crucial that the squad pay close attention to every word from the coach. Success often depends upon these mid-course alterations in strategy.

The great "halftime" of all ages was the cross of Christ, for human history has never been the same since the Savior died and rose again. Our Lord had several instructions for His men just before the suffering of Calvary. He predicted that they were going to suffer grief while the world rejoiced (v. 20). Then, He predicted great joy for His men when He arose from the dead (v. 22). Later, He predicted trouble in the world, but He promised the peace of God because of His victory over death and sin (v. 33). He knew all believers would need powerful resources for the "second half" after He returned to heaven.

His strategy for the final half concerned receiving God's resources through prayer. The disciples had prayed before but never in the name (based upon the merit) of the Lord Jesus. Now, because of the merit of Jesus and based on His work and will, we are told that we have access to God just as Jesus does (Romans 5:2). We can boldly approach the Father in Jesus' name to find help and answers in time of need (Hebrews 4:16). "In Jesus' name" is no magical phrase, but simply means that we are in agreement with His will and purpose. Therefore, we don't pray selfishly to indulge ourselves but are eager to glorify Him. The Father answers on the basis of His love for us. He is not obstinate; we don't need to beg to overcome a stubborn reluctance on His part. Realizing we stand before a living God so full of love should transform the way we pray.

Are you following the strategy for prayer that He outlined for the "second half" of time? Ask in His name as you agree with His purposes, and you'll surely receive. His game plans never fail.

Meditation Time-Out

1. What does it mean to ask "in His name"?
2. What is the basis of our access to God?
3. What is the basis of our peace in trying circumstances?

CONFERENCE
WITH THE COACH

Read John 17:1–5

"Father, the time has come. Glorify your Son, that your Son may glorify you."

John 17:1

M any coaches have been able to help their athletes through severe trials with wise counsel on such matters as grade problems, conflicts with a girlfriend, a nagging injury, or the player's role on the team. But the athlete must feel assured of the coach's concern and must express himself before such help can be given. At such troubled times in the lives of young people, the athlete's words usually reveal quite a bit about his character. If the desire in the heart of the player is wholesome and right, the problems are much more easily handled.

Though Jesus was a Master Coach Himself, He had to depend upon His heavenly Father in times of severe trial. His words in John 17 reveal His perfect desires and character. This chapter, correctly called "the Lord's Prayer" by some, contains seven requests as Jesus is facing the Cross. He prays for Himself, that He may glorify God (vv. 1–5). Then, He prays for His disciples, that they may be kept when He leaves (vv. 6–19). Finally, He prays for all future believers (vv. 20–26), that we may be one so that the world may believe in Him.

It is not wrong to pray for ourselves. Notice that this part of His prayer was the shortest—five verses—and was not self-centered but centered on the glory of God. Though God had promised to glorify His Son (John 12:28), Jesus prayed for it anyway. By praying in line with God's will, Jesus was sure of a positive answer. What a guide for our own prayers! It is not wrong to pray for blessing if our priority is the glory of God. However, being glorified in this case meant death on the cross. Suffering is not what we have in mind when we pray. Yet, it was essential to God's plan for the Lord Jesus, and it may be in His plan for us.

The truly righteous character of our Lord was revealed in His requests to God at the time of suffering. He glorified the Father by finishing the work given Him by the Father. Do you have that same attitude?

Meditation Time-Out

1. How did Jesus glorify God?
2. How did Jesus define *eternal life?*
3. How does God glorify Himself through you?

A SELFLESS AGENT

Read John 17:6–19

*"I pray for them. I am not pray-
ing for the world, but for those
you have given me, for they are
yours."*

John 17:9

T he structure of professional sports has been drastically altered by
the presence of agents who represent players in contract negotia-
tions and other matters. The agent intercedes on behalf of his clients and
looks out for their best interests. Though some agents are truly interested
in the player, many have selfish motives. Those who are only out for
themselves give agents a bad name.

Like an agent who protects those under him, Jesus Christ was especially concerned for the protection and preservation of His own. Verses
6–19 of John 17 vividly reveal His concern for His disciples and the
distinction He makes between the world (spoken of nineteen times in
this passage) and those given to Him out of the world. The world—
those who refuse to accept Christ and remain in the kingdom of darkness under the devil's control—hates believers in Christ because their
love for Him exposes its sham values (1 John 3:13). The world's desire
for pleasure, possessions, and power is a weak substitute for the
believer's love and devotion to the Lord Jesus (1 John 2:15–17). Our
Lord prayed first for the security of believers in a hostile world (John
17:11–12). He does not ask for the world to be preserved in its unbelief
but for the believers to be preserved. What a reason for comfort! Because we can't keep ourselves, the Master Coach keeps us. We did nothing to deserve our salvation and can do nothing to keep it. Indeed, if our

salvation depended upon our performance, we'd all be lost! Our security, our comfort, and our joy are provided by Him.

Jesus prayed for the disciples' singlemindedness in unity and in purpose (v. 11). As only a great coach can do, He took men of diverse backgrounds, loved them, taught them, and sent them out as a team to demonstrate the power of God. As on any team, unity is imperative.

Finally, Jesus prayed for the sanctification of the disciples (vv. 17–19). This means they were to be set apart for God's use in the world. They were not to be removed from the world (v. 15), but they were no longer to be of the world (v. 16). The Lord Himself was set apart to Calvary for our sakes that we might be set apart for Him.

Before leaving this planet, the Master Coach made sure of provisions for His players. His prayer for our security, singlemindedness, and sanctification is answered by the Father because He always prayed according to God's will. What comfort to be protected by the power of His name!

Meditation Time-Out

1. How do the world's values differ from the believer's values?
2. Why can believers never lose their salvation?
3. What does the term *sanctification* mean?

THE UNITY THAT SPEAKS

Read John 17:20–26

". . . that all of them may be one, Father, just as you are in me and I am in you."

John 17:21

More than one team has fallen short of its potential because of individual failures to sacrifice for one another. Never is lack of team cohesion more evident than in basketball, where five players must be screens for one another, pass to the open man, and switch assignments on defense. Conflicts over playing time, jealousy of a teammate's success, and rivalries over a girl have been known to disrupt team unity and curtail success. There must be a oneness on a winning team.

Jesus Christ, our Master Coach, knew that unity was essential for His team to succeed in its mission. In fact, He said it would be such an outstanding characteristic of His team that others would know they were believers in Him because of their mutual love (John 13:35).

Our Lord came to die for us, to be raised from the dead, and to return to heaven. He knew His mission would succeed. He knew the apostles would go everywhere telling people about Him and that millions of people would believe. So, before going back to His glory, He prayed for all future believers. This means He prayed for you and me before we were ever born. His prayer that we would be united as believers (v. 23), that we would one day be with Him in heaven (v. 24), and that we would see His glory (v. 24) will surely be answered, for He always prays according to the will of God.

The unity Jesus desires is an internal unity of heart and mind centered around the person of Christ. It is not external union centered around an organization. We should, therefore, be more eager to profess

Christ than to promote our church. All true believers have the same life, purpose, desires, and destiny. Yet, not all have the same temperaments, tastes, and manner of worship. Each organized church is made up of true believers and some who only profess to believe. We must promote our Lord, not our denomination! In the past, the great revivals of Luther and Wesley led to the formation of new churches because men realized that unity of mind around the Word of God was more vital than physical union in an organization. Today, the goal of a "one-world church" will fail because the organization behind it is not basing unity on God's Word.

All pettiness and harshness toward other believers must be abandoned as Christ draws His team together internally. His love for us is manifest by our love for each other. He hates the sowing of discord (Proverbs 6:16–19).

What is your attitude toward other believers? Do you secretly love gossip, dissension, and conflict? Are you one who sows such things? Or do you love other Christians as you love yourself? Do you seek ways to show your love by serving others? If you're truly on His team, you'll love your teammates as He did.

Meditation Time-Out

1. What three things did Jesus pray for all future believers?
2. How should the world recognize those who belong to Him?
3. Why is internal unity more important than an organization?

THE CUP OF
OUR SALVATION

Read John 18:1–14

"Shall I not drink the cup the Father has given me?"

John 18:11

R arely does a gymnast score a perfect 10, or even 9.5, on any routine in gymnastic competition. The standard is too high, the demands too rigid. The judge starts scoring as soon as the competitor walks onto the floor. He can deduct 3 points if he simply doesn't like the appearance or attitude of the athlete as he begins or concludes his routine.

Only one man has ever received a perfect ten from the heavenly Judge for His lifetime performance. That man was the Lord Jesus. His perfect performance, followed by His atoning death on Calvary, was totally acceptable to the Father. God loved us so much that He gave His Son this cup of suffering and death for us. Because the Son desired to please the Father, He drank every ounce of that cup.

It had already been a long, tiring day when Jesus went to a favorite place to pray, Gethsemane. There He was confronted by a cohort of Roman soldiers, about six hundred, along with temple police under Judas' direction. Though the Lord Jesus knew what was coming and had asked God to save mankind another way if possible, He walked out voluntarily to meet the angry mob (Matthew 26:39–44).

The center of all time is before the human race. Impulsive Peter draws a sword and takes a swipe at the head of one of the mob. Jesus stops him, for Almighty God doesn't need man's help in the struggle against sin. Twelve legions of angels, approximately seventy-two thousand, stood poised at the gate of heaven to invade at the nod of our Lord (Matthew 26:53). In 2 Kings 19:35, *one* death angel had slain 185,000 Assyrians in one night! Jesus could have obliterated humanity in one stroke and been completely justified. Knowing the soldiers' brutality, He also knew that Psalm 22, Psalm 69, Isaiah 50:5–7, and Isaiah 53 applied to Him, and He gave up His life for us. He was bound that we might go free.

At around midnight, Jesus was taken to Annas, whom Jewish writers acknowledge was the subtle power behind the corrupt priesthood. This was the first of six illegal trials—Jewish law forbade trials involving capital offenses to be held at night. The whole scene was staged quickly, according to plan, lest the murder interfere with the religious ritual of the Jewish weekend.

Our Lord faced it all alone for you and me. "As a sheep before her shearers is silent, so he did not open his mouth" (Isaiah 53:7). He totally pleased the heavenly Judge and made possible our salvation. What greater love could motivate our love and devotion to Him?

Meditation Time-Out

1. How did Jesus know what was coming?
2. Who was Jesus most concerned for during this arrest?
3. In what way did "drinking the cup" satisfy God?

FICKLE FOLLOWER

Read John 18:15–27

Again Peter denied it, and at that moment a rooster began to crow.

John 18:27

F ootball fans have a way of being fickle. They will boast enthusiastically about their team and coach and the success they expect. But let the same team and coach go through some rough times, and they get upset. Jerry Stovall, Dick Vermeil, and others could testify to that. Stovall was the 1982 SEC Coach of the Year and the Walter Camp Foundation Coach of the Year when his 8–3–1 LSU Tigers went to the Orange Bowl. But in 1983, the team's record was 4–7, and he was fired because his game plan was "inflexible." Vermeil was the Philadelphia Eagles' hero in 1980 when his team went to the Super Bowl, but became the fans' whipping boy in 1981 when the Eagles were eliminated. "Being in Philadelphia," he told the Associated Press, "I've found there's very little I have to gain [with the fans]. The only thing I can do is win the Super Bowl. Anything less, then I'm an idiot."

Before Pentecost, the Apostle Peter was a fickle follower of his Head Coach when the game plan didn't go as he expected. As Jesus let the mob arrest Him and His career seemed at the end, Peter's loyalty wavered. Though it was predicted by Jesus (John 13:38), Peter couldn't believe his own weakness. In fact, it was his self-confidence that precipitated his downfall. As he warmed himself at the enemy's fire (another mistake), in embarrassment about his association with Jesus he twice denied his Lord. The denial became vehement and took place over the space of a couple of hours (Mark 14:71). Finally a rooster crowed, marking the end of the third watch of the night, 3 A.M. Peter then caught a glimpse of his beaten Lord (Luke 22:61), remembered His words, and went out and wept bitterly in repentance (Luke 22:62). Remembering his complete failure later motivated Peter's rocklike trust in the Lord.

How loyal are you to the Master Coach? If His game plan does not suit you, do you backbite and criticize? Or are you like the person Peter later became—solid as a rock and willing to die for Him?

Meditation Time-Out

1. What circumstances led to Peter's denial?
2. What circumstances could lead you to deny Jesus?
3. In what ways have you denied your Lord?

MOCK TRIAL
OF RIGHTEOUSNESS

Read John 18:28–40

With this he went out again to the Jews and said, "I find no basis for a charge against him."

John 18:38

U ntil the final game of the 1972 Olympics, the USA had won all sixty-two basketball contests by an average margin of 26.2 points. With three seconds left, Doug Collins sank a pair of clutch free throws to apparently seal a 50–49 American victory over Russia to win the gold medal. Then came one of the most bitterly contested moments in Olympic history. *After* the Soviets had inbounded the ball, an official called time-out with one second left, because the Russians stormed the scorer's table and obstructed the view of the scorekeepers. Then, Dr. R. William Jones, secretary of the International Amateur Basketball Association, who had no authority in the matter, came out of the stands and ordered three seconds put back on the clock. Before the clock was reset, the Russians had inbounded the ball and missed a desperation shot. The USA went wild with joy. The clock was then reset, the ball inbounded by Yedesko (he stepped on the line in throwing it in), who threw to Belov (he was in the lane too long), who pushed a USA defender, and scored. Though eight international rules were violated at the game's conclusion, all protests were denied, the rules ignored, and the Soviets given the gold medal. The bitter memory of the event is still vivid in the minds of American sports fans.

The mockery of justice suffered by our Lord Jesus during six trials through the night and early morning is vivid in the courts of heaven also. No one came to His defense as Jesus was illegally tried, mocked, and beaten under the orders of the seventy-member Jewish Sanhedrin (Mark 14:55–64). False witnesses could not agree on the accusations against Him. Yet, at dawn, the death sentence was pronounced, and the Jews sent Him to the Romans, hoping they would carry it out. Concerned for ceremonial uncleanness, the Jews refused to enter Pilate's palace as they plotted murder. Pilate, the governor, heard the charges of sedition against Rome, knowing full well it was the envy of Jesus' popularity that motivated the Jewish religious leaders (Matthew 27:28). Attempting to avoid responsibility, he sent Jesus to Herod, who found Him innocent (Luke 23:6–12). Pilate appealed to the crowd which, under the influence of the priests, screamed for Jesus' blood. He offered to free a prisoner, and they chose Barabbas, a murderer. They preferred to have a sinner living next door than the One who could forgive their sins. Afraid of losing his position, Pilate chose political expediency over justice and gave in to the mob. The trial of Jesus really became a trial of Pilate, and his moral bankruptcy became evident.

Our sovereign Lord predicted all along what would happen (John 12:32–33). The injustice of human courts played into the hands of the spotless Lamb of God, who was killed in the prime of life on the Jewish Passover (Isaiah 53:8). The love and grace of God gave Him to us in innocence that we in our guilt might go free.

Meditation Time-Out

1. Why did the Jews need Pilate?
2. Who was responsible for the death of Jesus?
3. What kind of kingdom did Jesus rule?

THE MERCIFUL IN THE
HANDS OF THE MERCILESS

Read John 19:1–6

Then Pilate took Jesus and had him flogged. The soldiers twisted together a crown of thorns and put it on his head. . . . And they struck him in the face.

John 19:1, 3

V anderbilt University occasionally has a respectable football team, but that is not always the case. In the past, overwhelming defeats by scores of 66–3, 41–0, and 51–13 have humiliated both players and fans alike. As performance fell and scores rose against them, the bitterness of defeat stung more and more deeply. Sometimes teams would show mercy by heavy substitution, less passing, or refusing to add a field goal when all it would accomplish would be to run up the score.

The soldiers who mocked and tortured our Lord Jesus showed no such mercy. From daybreak until around 9 A.M. when He was crucified, brutal Roman soldiers mauled Jesus almost beyond recognition (Isaiah 52:14). They stripped Him, tied Him to a post, and beat Him repeatedly with whips made of short leather thongs studded with pieces of metal or bone. This Roman flogging was often fatal to the victim. They spit upon Him (Matthew 27:30), engaged in mock worship of the King of kings, and beat Him repeatedly. The crown of penetrating thorns on His head vividly pictured the burden of human sin which He bore in humiliation.

The whole scene was full of twisted irony. How ironic that the Great Physician was scourged that sick sinners might be healed. How ironic that though Pilate found Him innocent, he tortured Jesus anyway. His majestic calm through it all amazed the governor (John 19:9), and His claim of deity scared him (v. 8). How ironic also that the rebellious Jews chose Caesar over Christ, Rome over righteousness, a dictator over their Deliverer. They soon got all of Rome they wanted—the Romans leveled Jerusalem in A.D. 70.

Finally, how ironic that from the deepest imaginable suffering comes the greatest glory of God. Our Lord's humiliation reminds us of sin's degradation and God's wonderful love for us.

Meditation Time-Out

1. What kind of governor was Pilate?
2. What was the ultimate source of Pilate's authority?
3. What claim of Jesus struck fear in Pilate's heart?

SACRIFICED FOR US

Read John 19:17–27

Carrying his own cross, he went out to the place of the Skull (which in Aramaic is called Golgotha). Here they crucified him, and with him two others—one on each side and Jesus in the middle.

John 19:17–18

B aseball's squeeze bunt pictures exactly what took place when our Savior was sacrificed on the hill called Golgotha. As the pitcher delivers the ball, the runner on third breaks for home by faith that the bunter will sacrifice successfully. The batter gives up his "life" as a baserunner by bunting the ball to an infielder, who has no chance to throw out the sliding runner at home.

We should be so thankful that the Lord Jesus laid down the perfect sacrifice for mankind. The events leading up to His crucifixion were anything but pleasant. Around nine A.M., after a night of trial and torture, Jesus was loaded with a large beam and prodded down the streets of Jerusalem. The Roman stigma of "bearer of the cross" was added to His humiliation. Cicero, Rome's most famous orator, said, "Even the mere word, *cross,* must remain far not only from the lips of the citizens of Rome, but also from their thoughts, their eyes, their ears." Because of fatigue and blood loss, Jesus was unable to carry the load, probably a hundred pound beam to be fixed to an upright at the death site. Simon of Cyrene, a visitor in the crowd, was quickly drafted to help carry the cross. Upon arriving at the place of the Skull, the soldiers stripped Him, nailed His battered body to the beam, and raised Him to the sky. Ridiculed repeatedly by the crowd and mocked by the religious leaders, Jesus hung between heaven and earth for all men (Hebrews 2:9). Above His head, Pilate hung the sign, "Jesus of Nazareth, the king of the Jews." The sign was in three languages: Aramaic, the language of the common man; Latin, the language of the political rulers; and Greek, the language of the educated. Jesus was indeed crucified for the common man. He was crucified for those who nailed Him to the cross. And Jesus was crucified for the educated, for no matter how learned a man becomes he is still a sinner in need of a Savior.

All of us can truly see ourselves by looking at Jesus on the cross. The consequences of our sin become vivid as we recall His suffering. We deserved to be there. But because of His love for us, He became sin for us and died in our place (2 Corinthians 5:21). In perfect obedience to the "signals" from the Father, He suffered the shame of the cross (Philippians 2:8). Tongue or pen can never adequately describe the great sacrifice He made.

Meditation Time-Out

1. Why did the chief priests object to Pilate's sign?
2. What happened to Jesus' clothes?
3. Why are you thankful for Jesus' death?

FINISHING
WHAT HE STARTED

Read John 19:28–37

When he had received the drink, Jesus said, "It is finished." With that, he bowed his head and gave up his spirit.

John 19:30

Whether it means staying with a sport to the end of a tough season or giving 100 percent effort all the way through a game, finishing what one starts is an admirable character trait. Too often in our society, would-be athletes are tempted to quit when the going gets tough. The old slogan is true: "Many a man has bowed his head and left the dock just as his ship comes in."

We can thank God that our Lord Jesus never quit when the going was tough, for between the hours of twelve noon and 3 P.M. God, as Judge, turned His back on His only Son who became sin on behalf of His creation. For those three hours, the sun was blotted out as a sign of God's judgment on sin (Luke 23:44).

At 3 P.M., with a shout of triumph (*tetelestai*—"it is finished"), He bowed His head and willingly dismissed His Spirit. Ancient tax receipts with the word *tetelestai* written across the bill have been discovered indicating payment in full. Even in dying, He was in total control of the time and manner of His death. No man could take from Him what He voluntarily gave. He finished the fulfillment of all Old Testament prophecies of the suffering Savior. He finished the payment for all our sins. His death leaves nothing to be added to our salvation.

Simultaneous with His death, the thick temple veil separating God's Holy of Holies was split supernaturally from top to bottom. This occurred right during the evening sacrifice, so the Jewish priests would have seen what God did with their own eyes. An earthquake split the ground, and many believers were resurrected as further evidence of Christ's victory over the power of sin (Matthew 27:51–53).

Our Savior never let up. All the power of sin and Satan could not distract Him from His objective—a date with the Cross and the accomplishment of our salvation.

Meditation Time-Out

1. How does God react to sin?
2. What would have happened if Jesus had left the cross?
3. How do you know Jesus was dead?

SETTING THE STAGE

Read John 19:38–42

Because it was the Jewish day of Preparation and since the tomb was nearby, they laid Jesus there.

John 19:42

B efore victory is possible in a football game, there must be thorough preparation. There is a slogan that says, "Everyone has a will to win, but do you have the will to *prepare* to win?" Each player must be in physical condition; the plays must be memorized and practiced until they become automatic; and the team must stay within striking distance of its opponent late in the game. When these factors are present, the stage is set for victory.

A bold, rich man, Joseph of Arimathea, and an influential man, Nicodemus, set the stage for the greatest victory of all time by burying the body of Jesus. After the Romans certified His death following six hours of suffering on the cross, these formerly secret disciples now openly came forward to beg the body of the Lord from Pilate. They removed Jesus' body from the cross, bound it with linen sheets and seventy-five pounds of spices, and placed it in Joseph's garden tomb, a hollow in the side of a hill. Then they rolled a large flat stone across the entrance, which was sealed and heavily guarded (Matthew 27:66). It was a risky, expensive venture, and neither had anything personal to gain by identifying with the Lord.

The burial of our Savior marked the end of His suffering and humiliation. He is able to identify with all believers who die and are placed in the grave. But the most significant thing is that the stage was set for the greatest event in history, the glory of Easter morning when the greatest victory of all is celebrated!

Meditation Time-Out

1. Why was Jesus' burial significant?
2. What did the two men risk in asking for the body of our Lord?
3. Why do you think that, in God's providence, no one knows the exact site of Jesus' tomb today?

VICTORY FROM DEFEAT

Read John 20:1–9

Early on the first day of the week, while it was still dark, Mary Magdalene went to the tomb and saw that the stone had been removed from the entrance.

John 20:1

In 1980, the University of Georgia trailed Florida 21–19 with 1:32 remaining in a battle for a possible national championship. Stopped time and time again from deep in his own territory, quarterback Buck Belue was chased out of the pocket. It was third down with seventeen yards to go. Desperately, he rifled the ball over the middle, and Lindsay Scott leaped high to make the catch, broke to the open field, and raced ninety-three yards to pay dirt. No one has celebrated victory with greater enthusiasm than the Bulldogs celebrated in the end zone that day! Victory was truly snatched from defeat.

In the same way, Christ snatched victory for us from the very jaws of defeat. Mary Magdalene, from whom the Lord had cast seven demons (Luke 8:2), was among the first to discover conclusive proof of Jesus' great victory over sin and the grave. Arising while it was still dark, she headed for the tomb to anoint Jesus' body. When she arrived at the tomb, it was empty! An angel had rolled away the stone and sat upon it (Matthew 28:2). The sin and death that first became powerful in the Garden of Eden was now completely conquered in the garden where Christ arose from the dead. The empty tomb became the symbol of that victory, snatched from the very jaws of satanic defeat.

201

Just as our Lord's humiliation in death was great, His glorification was now greater. Mary, thinking someone had stolen the body, hurried to tell the disciples. She went first to Peter, who despite his recent denial of Jesus, was still recognized as leader of the timid group. When Peter and John reached the burial site, they, too, saw the evidence. This was no ordinary rabbi they had been following. He was everything He ever claimed to be—the Son of God and Savior of the world. His resurrection proved it, and the empty tomb became a memorial to the greatest victory in history.

Meditation Time-Out

1. Why was Mary heading for the tomb?
2. Where did she expect Jesus to be?
3. Why is the fact of the empty tomb significant?

AGONY AND ECSTASY

Read John 20:10–18

"Woman," he said, "why are you crying? Who is it you are looking for?"

John 20:15

T he Pittsburgh Steelers moved the ball steadily toward the goal line for the winning touchdown against the Browns. But Cleveland's defense stiffened, and on fourth and goal the Steelers were turned away in apparent defeat and utter dejection. Though very little time remained, the Pittsburgh defense held and forced a punt. With only fair field position and no time-outs, Terry Bradshaw hit pass after pass along the sidelines to kill the clock. Finally, on fourth and goal, he lofted a two-yard toss to Lynn Swan for the winning touchdown.

Sometimes our spiritual experience is like the highs and lows of a football game. It was that way for Mary Magdalene as she stood crying at Jesus' empty tomb. John had not yet told her of the Resurrection. But as she turned away from the angels, she recognized the voice of the Savior. He was right there in the midst of her deepest grief (Psalm 34:18). Her joy knew no bounds.

When she saw Him, Mary just had to share Him with others; she could not hoard the truth. Jesus told her to go tell His "brothers." He announced a new relationship to believers! Formerly, those who followed Him were "friends" (John 15:15). Now, for the first time He is not ashamed to call us "brothers" (Hebrews 2:11–12). Mary ran with great joy to tell the disciples (Matthew 28:8).

The greatest news ever announced spread quickly, and the joy of the resurrected Savior abounded everywhere. It filled the lives of the early believers so much that when meeting each other, one would say, "He is risen," to which the other would reply, "He is risen indeed!"

That same joy fills the hearts of true believers today, for the resurrection of the Lord Jesus gives hope in deepest grief and the promise that one day we will be with Him.

Meditation Time-Out

1. What were two angels doing at the tomb?
2. Why did Mary not immediately recognize Jesus?
3. How did Mary finally recognize Him?

THE RESURRECTION REVOLUTION

Read John 20:19–23

> . . . he showed them his hands and side. The disciples were overjoyed when they saw the Lord.
>
> John 20:20

When Ralph Houk managed the Yankees, occasionally a player would tire of the daily grind and ask to sit out a game. As *Reader's Digest* reports, Houk would say, "I know how you feel. Sure, take the day off. But do me a favor. You're in the starting lineup. Just play one inning. Then, skip the rest of the game." The player would follow Houk's instructions and most of the time get caught up in the spirit of the game and play until it was over.

On the evening of the first day of Jesus' resurrection, the disciples had no joy and were fearful for their lives. They were ready for a day off, possibly even thinking they had wasted three years following Jesus. Suddenly, Jesus Himself appeared physically among them, and their lives were never the same. Their gloom was changed to joy, their cowardice to boldness in sharing the news, their inner turmoil to perfect peace. They never thought of "sitting out" again.

Jesus Christ made at least fourteen physical appearances over forty days following His resurrection (Acts 1:3), once appearing to over five hundred people (1 Corinthians 15:3–6). He appeared five times that first day:

- to Mary Magdalene (Matthew 28:9)
- to the other women (Matthew 28:9)

- to Peter (Luke 24:33–35)
- on the road to Emmaus (Luke 24:13–32)
- and now at night to His disciples.

Though slow to believe, even determined not to believe, the disciples came to believe in spite of themselves. They touched Him, talked to Him, and ate with Him (Acts 10:41), proving that, though His was a glorified body capable of appearing and disappearing, He was present in flesh and bone. As a result of the proof of His resurrection, these feeble men went out and boldly told great numbers of people the truth about Jesus. Their transformation was so complete that all (except possibly John) were martyred for their conviction that He was alive. The drastic changes in the lives of His followers remain one of the greatest evidences for the Resurrection.

Meditation Time-Out

1. How did Jesus prove His identity to the disciples?
2. How were their lives changed after seeing Jesus?
3. How do you know Jesus is alive?

THAT YOU MAY BELIEVE

Read John 20:24–31

But these are written that you may believe that Jesus is the Christ, the Son of God, and that by believing you may have life in his name.

John 20:31

"Hammerin' Hank" Armstrong grew up homeless, penniless, and alone. Born in a Mississippi city slum, he lived life as a hobo and attended the school of hard knocks. Eventually, his powerful fists won him fame and fans. In 1937, as a pro boxer, he beat Petey Sasson to become Featherweight Champion of the World. He became convinced that God had given him the title for a purpose—to gain a hearing for the Word of God. Months later, he took on the great Barney Ross and defeated him for the Welterweight Championship. Then, in 1938, in one of boxing's bloodiest fights, he decisioned Lou Ambers in fifteen rounds for the World's Lightweight Championship. Hank Armstrong became the first and only man in history to own three world championships at the same time. He now had gained his hearing.

Two thousand years ago, Jesus did something that gained Him an even greater hearing. He rose bodily from the dead. Edersheim, a historian, called Christ's resurrection the "best established fact in history." Ewald said, "Nothing is more historically certain than that Jesus rose from the dead and appeared again to His followers." Of the four major world religions based upon a person (all others are based upon a philosophy), only Christianity has a resurrected founder. Abraham, the father of the Jews, died about 1900 B.C., and no one claimed he was resurrected. The Mahaparinbbana Sutta, which contains the earliest accounts

207

of Buddah's death, records that he died "with that utter passing away in which nothing whatever remains behind." Mohammed died on June 8th, A.D 632., and his tomb is still occupied and visited annually.

The gospel writers were eyewitnesses and had more evidence to prove Jesus' claim to deity than they could record (John 21:25). John tells of one appearance to a doubting Thomas. Though Thomas was a skeptic and possibly a loner, Jesus didn't chide him for being absent at the last meeting. He presented Himself again and Thomas believed. Jesus' resurrection had gained another hearing and another heart.

Meditation Time-Out

1. Why do you think Thomas doubted the Resurrection?
2. Why do some people not believe in Jesus today?
3. Why can we accept the accounts of the Gospel writers as accurate?

FANATICAL FOR JESUS

Read John 21:1–14

As soon as Simon Peter heard him say, "It is the Lord," he wrapped his outer garment around him (for he had taken it off) and jumped into the water.

John 21:7

Sometimes people become fanatics for their favorite team. Take, for example, the Detroit fans who went completely berserk when the 1984 Tigers won the World Series. Or the Florida football fan who, before his death in 1982, requested that the next time the Gators defeated Georgia, someone would put a copy of the sports page facedown on his grave. (The guy's best friend actually did it when the Gators won in 1984). Or the Nebraska Cornhusker fan who requested that when he died, they drop his ashes from the sky into Memorial Stadium in Lincoln during a home game.

Seven disciples were anything but fanatics when they returned to fishing after the resurrection of Jesus. They were confused and unsure of the future. To top it off, they fished all night and caught nothing. As morning dawned, Jesus (though unrecognized) called from shore, asking whether they had caught anything. It is hard for a fisherman to admit failure and though not wanting to discuss it, they replied, "No." Then He instructed them to cast on the right of the boat. They obeyed and reaped a great harvest. Suddenly, they recognized the Lord, and Peter became fanatical. He left the boat and swam to the Savior. The others followed. Jesus calmly cooked breakfast, and they basked in His presence once again. They became lifetime fanatics of the Lord Jesus, each willing to die for the One who loved and cared for him.

Service in our own strength is always fruitless. But, directed by the Master and done in the resurrection power of Jesus Christ, great fruit results. That power is available to us today, for Jesus indwells all believers. He was given all authority in heaven and on earth (Matthew 28:18). We have a Savior worthy of our fanatical devotion.

Meditation Time-Out

1. What goals did Jesus' disciples have before Jesus reappeared?
2. How did Jesus approach His floundering followers?
3. What would you say to one who called you fanatical about Jesus?

CONFIDENCE IN
THE QUARTERBACK

Read John 21:15–25

Then he said to him, "Follow me!"

John 21:19

I n the glamour of Kenny Anderson's greatest season as Cincinnati's quarterback (1981), the first quarter he played that year has long been forgotten. In the Bengals' opener against Seattle, Anderson completed five of fifteen passes for thirty-nine yards and two interceptions, and his team fell behind 21–0. Coach Forrest Gregg replaced Kenny with rookie Turk Schonert, who had never played in the NFL. Schonert rallied the team to a 27–21 victory, and Gregg seriously considered starting him the following week. But, refusing to give up on Anderson, he came back to him when the Bengals played against New York. The coach's faith in his star paid off. Anderson allowed only eight more interceptions in the next sixty-three quarters and won the AFC Most Valuable Player award.

Peter was so glad and so humbled to discover that Jesus never gave up on him, either. Just prior to His ascension, when He would be taken to heaven before their eyes (Acts 1:9), our Lord had a heart-to-heart talk with the man who had denied Him three times. Peter's denials had taken place in the courtyard beside a fire; Jesus now rebuilt his confidence by a fire on the shores of the Sea of Galilee. The Savior asked, "Do you love (*Agape,* the strongest form of love) Me?" Peter only dared reply, "Yes, Lord, I love (*Phileo,* friendship type of love) You." The man who had once boasted he would never desert the Lord Jesus had no more confidence in his commitment. His boasting was now a thing of the past.

211

Yet, Peter responded as Jesus expressed a desire to use him anyway. After directing him to "feed my sheep," our Lord invited Peter to "follow Me." Peter's devotion lasted a lifetime, and tradition says he was eventually crucified upside down as a martyr for the Savior.

Thank God He never gives up on us! He promises to be with us always (Matthew 28:20), and our Lord was not given to idle words! No matter how we fail, the Master Coach is quick to encourage us. When He returns us to the game, the results are often multiplied!

Meditation Time-Out

1. What is the proper motive for service to Christ?
2. How has God recently encouraged you?
3. What indication does John give that Jesus will return to earth?

ABOUT
THE AUTHORS

E lliot Johnson is a teaching assistant at Middle Tennessee State University. He has been a college head baseball coach for twelve years and currently assists the MTSU team. He is the director for the Winning Run Foundation and president of Johnson Baseball Enterprises.

Elliot Johnson and his wife Judy reside in Antioch, Tennessee, with their two sons, Todd and Benjamin.

Al Schierbaum graduated from Dallas Baptist University in 1982 and then went to Criswell Bible College and obtained a Master's degree in Biblical Studies. Al coached Athletes In Action teams during the summers of 1986 and 1988.

Al Schierbaum is presently a part-time professor in the Religion Department, assistant baseball coach (pitching), and chaplain at Dallas Baptist University in Dallas, Texas.

The typeface for the text of this book is *Times Roman*. In 1930, typographer Stanley Morison joined the staff of *The Times* (London) to supervise design of a typeface for the reformatting of this renowned English daily. Morison had overseen type-library reforms at Cambridge University Press in 1925, but this new task would prove a formidable challenge despite a decade of experience in paleography, calligraphy, and typography. *Times New Roman* was credited as coming from Morison's original pencil renderings in the first years of the 1930s, but the typeface went through numerous changes under the scrutiny of a critical committee of dissatisfied *Times* staffers and editors. The resulting typeface, *Times Roman*, has been called the most used, most successful typeface of this century. The design is of enduring value to English and American printers and publishers, who choose the typeface for its readability and economy when run on today's high-speed presses.

Substantive Editing:
Michael S. Hyatt

Copy Editing:
Susan Kirby

Cover Design:
Steve Diggs & Friends
Nashville, Tennessee

Page Composition:
Xerox Ventura Publisher
Linotronic L-100 Postscript® Imagesetter

Printing and Binding:
Lake Book Manufacturing, Inc.
Melrose Park, Illinois

Cover Printing:
Lake Book Manufacturing, Inc.
Melrose Park, Illinois